FOCUS
International Economics

WRITING TEAM

Gerald J. Lynch, *Chair*

Michael W. Watts

Donald R. Wentworth

CONTRIBUTING AUTHORS

Harlan Day

Jane Lopus

Charles Noussair

Caryn Kikta

Daniel Vazzanna

The National Council on Economic Education gratefully acknowledges funding of this project received from the following sources:

- The U.S. Department of Education, through a grant from the Office of Educational Research and Improvement, PR #R304A70001.

- The Purdue University Center for International Business Education and Research (CIBER)

- The Indiana Council for Economic Education

National Council
on Economic Education

THE EconomicsAmerica AND EconomicsInternational PROGRAMS

AUTHORS

Gerald J. Lynch
Associate Professor of Economics
Purdue University

Michael W. Watts
Professor of Economics
Director, Center for Economic Education
Purdue University

Donald R. Wentworth
Professor of Economics and Education
Director, Center for Economic Education
Pacific Lutheran University

CONTRIBUTING AUTHORS
Harlan Day
Executive Director, Indiana Council for Economic Education
Purdue University

Jane Lopus
Associate Professor of Economics
Director, Center for Economic Education
California State University, Hayward

Charles Noussair
Associate Professor of Economics
Purdue University

Caryn Kikta
Purdue University

Daniel Vazzanna
Purdue University

The National Council on Economic Education gratefully acknowledges the funding of this publication by the U.S. Department of Education, Office of Educational Research and Improvement, under PR Grant #R304A70001. Any opinions, findings, conclusions, or recommendations expressed in this publication are those of the authors and do not necessarily reflect the view of the U.S. Department of Education.

ISBN 1-56183-496-3

5 4 3

CONTENTS

FOREWORD

Focus: International Economics is the latest volume in a new generation of National Council on Economic Education (NCEE) publications, dedicated to increasing the economic literacy of all students. The *Focus* publications, the centerpiece of NCEE's comprehensive **Economics-America** program, build on almost five decades of success in delivering economic education to America's students.

The *Focus* series is innovative, using economics to enhance learning in subjects such as history, geography, civics, and personal finance, as well as economics. Activities are interactive, reflecting the belief that students learn best through active, highly personalized experiences with economics. Applications of economic understanding to real-world situations and contexts dominate the lessons. In addition, the lessons are correlated to NCEE's *Voluntary National Content Standards in Economics* and *A Framework for Teaching the Basic Economic Concepts*.

Focus: International Economics highlights and examines basic concepts and issues in international economics. The 20 lessons presented are organized around several major content themes: international economics, global production and competition, exchange rates and issues in international finance, free trade vs. protectionism, international economic development, and economic systems. Student activities focus on such topics as: why people and nations trade, interpreting trade data, trade barriers, balance of payments, where to locate a factory, foreign currency and exchange rates, should developing countries have free trade, the debate over NAFTA, and privatization around the world.

The development of this publication was undertaken as part of the International Education Exchange program funded by the United States Department of Education, Office of Educational Research and Improvement under PR Grant #R304A70001. The National Council on Economic Education extends its deep appreciation to the Department of Education for its support of this program, in particular, OERI program officer, Dr. Ram Singh. We are also grateful that the United States Congress had the foresight to realize the need for economic education in the emerging market economies and the vision to see how an international exchange program such as this could benefit U.S. students and teachers.

Support for the development of this publication was also provided by the Purdue University Center for International Business and Education Research, and the Indiana Council for Economic Education. NCEE gratefully acknowledges their contribution.

The National Council thanks the authors, Gerald J. Lynch, Associate Professor of Economics, Purdue University, who took the lead on this project, and his co-authors: Michael W. Watts, Professor of Economics, and Director, Center for Economic Education, Purdue University; Donald R. Wentworth, Professor of Economics and Education, and Director, Center for Economic Education, Pacific Lutheran University; Harlan Day, Executive Director, Indiana Council for Economic Education, Purdue University; Jane Lopus, Associate Professor of Economics, and Director, Center for Economic Education, California State University, Hayward; Charles Noussair, Associate Professor of Economics, Purdue University; Caryn Kikta, Purdue University; and Daniel Vazzanna, Purdue University.

Robert F. Duvall, Ph.D.
President and CEO
National Council on Economic Education

ACKNOWLEDGMENTS

The writing team of *Focus: International Economics* would like to thank the members of the writing team of the forerunner of this edition, the *Master Curriculum Guide in Economics: Teaching Strategies, International Trade*. While we have updated much of the material to reflect interests in international economics and finance as they exist today, the basic format and approach were drawn from the *MCG*. The members of the first writing team were Donald R. Wentworth and Kenneth E. Leonard (with contributions from Norris Peterson, Ernest Ankrim, Robert Jensen, and David Vinje), all of Pacific Lutheran University.

Initial support for this publication came from Purdue University. We would like to thank the Purdue University Center for International Business Education and Research (CIBER) and its director, Professor Marie Thursby, and the Indiana Council for Economic Education and its past director, Peter Harrington, and its present director, Harlan Day, for their assistance.

Through its EconomicsInternational program, the National Council on Economic Education received major financial support for this publication through a grant from the Office of Educational Research and Improvement, United States Department of Education.

We also thank the following teachers who field-tested or otherwise assessed drafts of the various lessons in this book:

David Ballard, Indiana Department of Education

Janet Carlson, Ygnacio Valley High School, Concord, California

Steve Caziarc, Alameda High School, Alameda, California

Leslie Davidson, Indiana Department of Education

Jody Healy, Roosevelt Middle School, Twin Lakes School Corporation, Indiana

Jeff Knoy, McCutcheon High School, Tippecanoe School Corporation, Lafayette, Indiana

Chris McGrew, Carroll Junior-Senior High School, Carroll Consolidated School Corporation, Indiana, and Indiana Department of Education

Sally Petro, Martin T. Krueger Junior High School, Michigan City Area Schools, Indiana

Jeanne Vander Ploeg, Castilleja School, Palo Alto, California

We received excellent secretarial help from JoEllen Hayworth who, after many years of working around economic education, has returned to school to be a teacher. Her able assistance will be missed, but we wish her much luck. Julie Huffer also provided secretarial assistance and special assistance with the graphs. At the National Council, the encouragement of Robert Duvall and the prodding and direction of Barb DeVita made this project move along more quickly than it would have without some gentle nagging. All of us thank the many students we have taught over the years whose quizzical looks let us know that we weren't really communicating very well and needed to think of new approaches for instruction. It is primarily for the students that this book is written.

INTRODUCTION

The first edition of this volume was published in 1988, and since then international economics has become an even more important part of daily life for consumers, firms, and governments all over the world. Levels of world trade have increased dramatically. Free trade agreements and increased competition from foreign companies have become major political issues in many national elections. Concerns about recent trends in standards of living are reflected in media reports, academic studies, and discussions or arguments with family members and friends. The sudden collapse of the former Soviet bloc and the often tentative and uneven steps toward market reforms in those former command economies have serious implications for U.S. security and public policy interests, and major economic implications as those large new markets become accessible to Western firms. For all of these reasons, it is now commonplace to hear or read reports about the U.S. balance of trade and balance of payments, and the strength or weakness of the dollar against other national currencies.

Unfortunately, most students, teachers, and citizens know even less about concepts and issues in international economics than they do about economics in general. This volume can help teachers fill those gaps. The lessons in this volume are grouped under several major content themes, which are briefly explained below.

A WORLD OF GLOBAL CONSUMERS

Virtually all U.S. consumers buy goods made in other nations, and many travel to other countries on business or as tourists. Spending by U.S. consumers, firms, and government agencies for goods and services produced in other countries makes up our national imports. On the other hand, many firms, other organizations, and consumers from other nations, including people who travel to the United States on business or as tourists, buy goods and services produced here. That spending represents U.S. exports.

Sometimes the items imported into this country can not be produced here because certain productive resources are not available in the United States. More frequently, imports are things that might be produced in this country but are not, or things that were once produced here but no longer are. In other cases, the imported goods are products that are also currently produced in the United States, and so the imports compete directly with domestically produced goods. There are also products that were once produced only in other countries that are now produced in this country as well. In the markets for those products, domestic producers once again compete directly with foreign producers.

As consumers, people maximize the level of satisfaction they can achieve, given their limited incomes, by purchasing the products that give them the most satisfaction per dollar, usually without regard to where those products were produced. Unless the fact that a product was produced in another country is itself important to consumers' preferences, they will not consider a product's country of origin in deciding what to buy. There are some situations where consumers do care about buying products made in certain countries. For example, a visitor may want to buy a souvenir while traveling in another country, or consumers may believe that products from some countries are of higher quality than products from other countries. On the other hand, some people feel that it is patriotic to buy products made in their own nation. But those cases are exceptions, not the rule.

In the United States, it turns out that most spending is accounted for by goods and services made in this country (that is, the purchase of domestically produced goods makes up the bulk of GDP). But that is true because it generally is not practical to buy housing and most services (including health care, education, food at restaurants, and maintenance work on houses, cars, and major appliances) from foreign producers, not because U.S. consumers deliberately try to avoid products made in other countries. In fact, over the last few decades, spending for imports in this country has risen dramatically, both in terms of real dollars (adjusted for inflation), and as a percentage of overall levels of national income. Not coincidentally, the level of U.S. exports has also risen sharply over this same period.

GLOBAL PRODUCTION AND COMPETITION AMONG THE MANY

When consumers are free to buy whatever they want from a wide range of producers competing for the consumer's business, the result is a very efficient system of production and trade. The idea of economic efficiency has two distinct meanings: first, producing the things consumers want most, and second, producing goods and services of a given quality level at the lowest possible cost and selling them at the lowest possible price. Having more products and producers for consumers to choose from tends to support both of these outcomes in any given market at any given time. Where there are many relatively small firms selling identical products, prices are driven down to the costs of production, including only a "normal" level of profit that is just high enough to keep producers active in these markets. International trade is an important way of increasing the level of competition in some markets, because it adds to the number of producers competing for consumers' business. It also increases the variety of products available to consumers around the world.

For these reasons, allowing producers from all over the world to sell their products in any countries they choose to strikes many people as a good, commonsense idea. It is, in fact, an idea that the great majority of professional economists have long supported, starting with the person widely regarded as the first professional economist, Adam Smith. Smith and later economists developed formal theories and a lot of empirical evidence to show that free trade among nations moves the production of goods and services to places where products can be produced at the lowest opportunity cost. In other words, the production of textiles, automobiles, airplanes, and other goods that are traded internationally will be concentrated in countries where resources are especially well suited to the production of those products, and where the value of what must be given up to produce those products is lowest. In economics, this is known as the principle of comparative advantage.

While the specific calculation of comparative advantage is a bit complex, there are, fortunately, many applications of the idea at work that students have seen all their lives and can understand intuitively. One example involves an attorney who happens to be a better typist than his or her secretary. Why would the attorney hire someone else to do typing that the attorney could do faster? Because time spent typing is generally time not spent doing more valuable legal work. That means the opportunity cost of having the attorney type is very high, so the attorney specializes in legal work, the typist specializes in typing, and they both rely on thousands of other specialized workers and companies to provide the other goods and services they buy and consume. By specializing and trading, the overall production (and therefore consumption) of all goods and services, including both typing and legal services, can be increased.

International specialization and trade is, fundamentally, no different from the attorney-secretary example. It sometimes looks different, because products must cross political borders, and two or more national currencies and languages may be involved. But the factors that lead different workers or regions in one nation to specialize in production, and trade with many others to get the things they want to consume, are the precisely the same factors that lead to international specialization and trade. And just as in the attorney-secretary example, even large, wealthy nations often find it in their own best interests to specialize in the production of some things and trade for many others even when the trading partner is smaller, poorer, and weaker in the production a given product. For example, if it chose to do so, the United States could grow more coffee beans than are grown today in South America by using greenhouses to control temperature and humidity for the coffee plants. But that would cost much more than buying the coffee beans from countries where the climate is well suited for growing the beans, and where workers have fewer opportunities than U.S. workers to get high-paying jobs in factories or in professional careers. So, like the attorney who hires a typist, the United States finds it too costly to use its resources to make things that can be produced at a lower opportunity cost in other nations.

Of course, those cost savings have to be large

enough to cover any costs of getting the products from one person to another, or from one country to another in the case of international trade, before it pays to specialize and trade. But transportation costs are a small part of the total production costs for most goods, and in most countries people and organizations specialize in producing only a few things—far fewer than the number of things they consume. That wasn't always true, as in the pioneer days when people lived too far away from others to trade very often and had to be largely self-sufficient. But economic growth and progress allowed countries to develop roads, ports, transportation systems, and markets. Specialization and increasing levels of interdependence, both within countries and internationally, have been an integral part of that growth and progress.

How people and countries specialize depends on the mix of productive resources and the level of skills they have. These factors change over time as people and organizations in different countries use up some resources (such as oil and deposits of other natural resources) and develop others (such as capital and labor resources, by investing in capital and the education and training of workers). Different nations are endowed with different quantities and combinations of natural resources, and over time they make different investments in capital goods and in the education and training of human resources. Different economic systems also provide different incentives and rewards to successful investors and entrepreneurs. All of these differences help to explain why, today or at any given point in time, the level of capital and the level of education and skills for labor vary so much across nations. Those different levels of capital and human capital resources in turn play a major role in explaining the patterns of international specialization, interdependence, and trade, and also the different national levels of output and standards of living.

MONEY, EXCHANGE RATES AND ISSUES IN INTERNATIONAL FINANCE

To buy goods and services from another country, a buyer in the United States must change dollars into the currency of the other nation. In turn, people from other countries are willing to sell their currency for dollars because they want to use those

dollars to buy goods and services produced in the United States. What that means, in real terms, is that we ultimately pay for goods and services from other countries by sending goods and services produced in this country to our trading partners.

But in practice, the people and organizations that import goods and services from other countries are often not the same as those that export goods and services to pay for those imports. If they were, the system of international trade would operate essentially as a system of direct barter, and it is well known that barter is a clumsy and inefficient system of trading, compared to using money. International trade requires the use of money from two or more countries, and that leads to specialized markets where people buy and sell the currencies of different countries.

Even at banks that operate a small "window" or department for trading international currencies, it is easy to find examples that illustrate how this currency trading is based on a few key types of exchange. Some people buy foreign currencies with dollars because they are making trips abroad as tourists or on business. Others buy foreign currencies with dollars to pay for business transactions with foreign producers and organizations, even though they may not have traveled to other countries. On the other side of the market, foreign tourists who come to the United States buy dollars with their national currencies, as do foreign firms and other organizations that buy U.S. products. In doing that, they supply the foreign currency that is sold for dollars, just as U.S. tourists and businesses were supplying dollars in exchange for foreign currencies.

Banks and other "middlemen" in international currency markets provide a service to their customers by making it easier for those buyers and sellers of dollars and foreign currencies to find each other. Banks do this to earn a small commission on the transaction, as shown in the difference between *buy* and *sell* columns on signs or printed tables that list exchange rates for different currencies.

If the demand for a nation's currency rises faster than the supply of its currency in foreign exchange markets, owing to increased demand for that nation's exports or capital resources, or both, then the value of that nation's currency will rise (appreciate) relative to other nations' currencies. That has the effect of making the nation's exports and capital resources more expensive to people in other countries, and over time these adjustments in exchange rates help to balance a nation's imports and exports. If the supply rises faster than the demand, the value of a nation's currency will fall (depreciate) on the foreign exchange market.

Exchange rates are also affected by changes in a nation's monetary and fiscal policies. *(Monetary policies* refers to changes in a nation's supply of money and availability of credit; *fiscal policies* refers to changes in a national government's spending and tax policies.) These macroeconomic stabilization policies can sometimes influence national levels of output, unemployment, and inflation, at least in the short run. Some of these policies can also affect the exchange rate for the nation's currency in ways that offset the intended expansionary or contractionary effects of the policies, by affecting the demand for the nation's exports. For example, one variable that influences exchange rates, and is influenced by a nation's monetary and fiscal policies, is interest rates. Rising (real) interest rates in a nation will increase the demand for that nation's currency, other things being equal, as savers and investors from other nations open savings accounts and buy bonds and other interest-bearing securities from that country, to earn the higher interest rates. A higher price for the nation's currency will reduce the demand for its exports, other things being equal. That will support the goals of a contractionary monetary policy, which might have been responsible for the higher interest rates. But it will work against the goals of expansionary fiscal policies, which can also lead to higher interest rates.

Because the levels of spending for imports, exports, and investments in real and financial capital assets by people in different countries can affect the overall performance of national economies in these ways, the spending flows are regularly tabulated and reported each year in what are called balance of payments accounts.

FREE TRADE VS. PROTECTIONISM, AND FREE TRADE AGREEMENTS AND ORGANIZATIONS

Although voluntary trade between people and organizations in different countries increases overall production and consumption levels, some firms and workers can be hurt by increased competition from foreign producers when the level of international trade increases. (Note that the same thing often happens when a new domestic firm enters a market to compete with old, established firms. But that competition is more widely accepted as a good thing, even when the firms and workers affected by domestic competition are the same ones that would be hurt by competition from foreign producers.)

Firms and workers facing increased competition from foreign producers naturally find it strongly in their interests to seek government protection in the form of tariffs, quotas, or other trade restrictions. These trade barriers hurt consumers, since they will have to pay higher prices for both foreign and domestic products in these markets. Trade barriers also reduce a nation's exports over time (hurting firms and workers in those industries), because the dollars spent on imported goods are typically decreased by the trade restrictions, which means people in those nations have fewer dollars to spend on U.S. products.

To overcome the special-interest problems that lead to restrictions on international trade, a number of agreements and organizations supporting free trade globally or among countries from certain regions of the world have been established over the past 50 years. The results of these initiatives have been generally favorable in terms of increasing worldwide production and consumption levels, although some of the regional trading blocs (such as the European Union) promote free trade within the bloc but restrict trade with other countries. For that reason, the truly global trading agreements and organizations, such as the World Trade Organization (WTO), have been particularly important in promoting freer international trade among all countries, and in making regional trading agreements more beneficial by limiting the restrictions they can impose on non-member countries.

That does not mean that everyone supports free-trade initiatives. In fact, in the United States they have proven to be controversial political issues near-ly every time the President considers signing or the Senate considers ratifying such treaties. Much of the opposition stems from special interest groups representing firms and workers wanting to limit the competition they face. Some of it develops because many people do not understand that reducing imports hurts consumers and exporters. In some special cases, issues such as national defense, or market power on the part of large foreign firms or cartels, or the key role of high tech industries and their effect on production and consumption levels in many other industries, have led some economists to support trade restrictions in a few particular markets.

INTERNATIONAL ECONOMIC DEVELOPMENT AND THE CONVERGENCE OR DIVERGENCE OF LIVING STANDARDS IN DIFFERENT NATIONS

The market value of all final goods and services produced in an economy in one year is known as that nation's Gross Domestic Product (GDP). GDP is primarily used to measure business cycles and out-put fluctuations, not living standards. However, while it is admittedly an imperfect measure of material living standards, real per capita GDP, which adjusts GDP to account for the number of people in a nation and any inflation that occurs over time, is still the most widely used and proba-bly the best available single measure of the average standard of living in different nations.

Economic growth is measured by increases in real per capita GDP over time. How large a nation's GDP can be is determined by the available quantity and quality of its natural, human, and capital resources. To increase real per capita GDP over time typically requires investments in both physical capital (such as factories and machines) and human capital (the education, training, skills, and health of a nation's labor force).

High wages and living standards in industrialized nations are based on high per capita levels of out-put of goods and services. These high levels of labor productivity are in turn supported by past investments in physical and human capital. Among

nations that make substantial investments in physi-cal and human capital, there is a tendency for liv-ing standards to converge. In other words, the nations that are not the most prosperous of these developed nations tend to catch up by growing faster than those that are more prosperous. Convergence happens partly because higher labor payments in the most prosperous nations make it profitable to move some kinds of production and jobs to countries where workers have the necessary skills to do the same work but receive lower wages and salaries, and partly because the technological knowledge and methods developed in the wealthiest countries are often transferred quickly to other countries.

In countries that have not made substantial investments in physical and human capital and are not richly endowed with natural resources, average living standards have remained very low, often below official U.S. poverty levels.

ECONOMIC SYSTEMS—MARKET ECONOMIES VS. CENTRAL PLANNING, AND THE TRANSITION ECONOMIES OF EASTERN EUROPE AND ASIA

Human wants exceed the capacity to produce goods and services to satisfy those wants. This probably will always be the case. That means that all resources have alternative uses, so some method must be adopted to determine which goods and ser-vices will be produced with available resources, how those goods and services will be produced, and who will consume those goods and services. Taken together, the methods used to answer those basic economic questions constitute a nation's economic system. The three basic economic systems used throughout history have been market economies, central planning economies, and traditional economies.

Market economies feature private ownership of goods, services, and productive resources, including capital resources. Consumers and producers are free to choose what to buy and sell, and their inter-action in different markets establishes prices that serve as key signals and incentives to encourage or discourage the production and consumption of dif-ferent things. No central planning agency is required to determine the quantity of different things to be produced, or the prices of these goods and services.

In central planning systems, political rulers or designated committees and experts determine production and consumption levels for different goods and services, and they set official prices for products administratively. Since about 1989, most of the central planning economies in the world, which were formerly part of the Soviet bloc, have begun a transition process toward market economies. This effort has required massive privatization and other institutional reforms, often accompanied by at least temporary periods of inflation and decreased national output.

Today, some of these countries have made substantial progress in moving toward market systems, and they are experiencing rapid economic growth. Some other countries have not moved as quickly or as far in the direction of markets. Many people in these countries are enduring severe economic hardship, particularly the elderly who no longer receive adequate government pensions. Most U.S. economists feel that the transition economies will require much more time to converge with living standards in the industrialized market economies; but it is also widely recognized that the old central planning systems were extremely inefficient, and delivered much lower living standards than the Western market economies.

WHY DO PEOPLE TRADE?

INTRODUCTION

Most international trade is the voluntary exchange of goods and services between individuals and businesses located in different countries. Nations do not trade. Instead, individuals representing nations, individuals representing businesses, and individuals representing themselves make trading decisions. Voluntary trades are made when both parties expect to gain from the trade. Such trades may continue in the future if both parties are pleased with the exchange. If the consequences of trading are not satisfactory, then the parties will not continue their voluntary trade.

People evaluate their satisfaction from trades by weighing the costs and the benefits they receive from the trades. How much do they value what they give up? How much do they value what they receive? When the expected benefits outweigh the expected costs, people trade. When the expected costs outweigh the expected benefits, people don't trade.

CONCEPTS
Trade
Voluntary exchange
Costs
Benefits

CONTENT STANDARDS

Voluntary exchange occurs only when all participating parties expect to gain. This is true for trade among individuals or organizations within a nation, and among individuals or organizations in different nations.

Exchange is trading goods and services with people for other goods and services or for money.

The oldest form of exchange is barter the direct trading of goods and services between people.

When people buy something, they value it more than it costs them; when people sell something, they value it less than the payment they receive.

OBJECTIVES
◆ Identify the expected costs of a voluntary trade.
◆ Identify the expected benefits of a voluntary trade.
◆ Distinguish between a voluntary and involuntary trade.
◆ Explain how value is created, and overall satisfaction increases, when people trade.

LESSON DESCRIPTION
Students participate in a trading activity. In a debriefing session, they discuss their actions and compare their behavior with trading behavior that occurs in the economy.

TIME REQUIRED
One class period.

MATERIALS
★ One transparency each of Visuals 1, 2, and 3
★ Pencils and paper for students
★ One small paper bag per student, containing one or more tradable item(s) such as dried fruit, small boxes of raisins, pencils, stickers, library passes, shampoo, soap, etc. Make the bags very different from one another. For example, prepare some bags containing unpopular items, only a single item, many of the same items, many different items, items more popular with boys, and items more popular with girls.

PROCEDURE
1. Explain to the students that they will investigate trading behavior today by participating in a trading activity and by using that experience to learn more about international trade.

2. Display Visual 1, **Why Do People Trade?** Ask students to answer this question and put their responses on the chalkboard. Treat these

responses as hypotheses that will be tested against the evidence developed in the rest of the activity.

3. Put students in groups of three, and tell them to take out a pencil and sheet of paper.

4. Distribute the bags containing tradable items to the students, one bag per student. Tell them not to look in the bags until you give them permission.

5. Tell the students to look into their bags without showing the contents to other students, and to rate their bag contents on a scale of 1-5. (One is the lowest rating; five is the highest.) Ask the students to write down their rating on their sheet of paper.

6. Let the students take items out of the bag and show them to other people in the group, if they choose to do so.

7. Allow the students two minutes to trade items WITHIN THEIR GROUP OF THREE, if they can agree on a trade. No one is required to make a trade.

8. After the two-minute trading session, ask the students who have made a trade to raise their hands. Write down the total number of trades on the chalkboard. Then ask the students to give examples of trades they made, and trades they did not agree to make, so that other students get some idea of what tradable items are available in the entire class.

9. Ask the students to rate the item(s) they now have on a scale of 1-5. See how many students report a higher score after trading, how many report the same score, and how many (if any) a lower score. *(People who traded are likely to give the new item(s) a higher rating. Some people who did not trade may also change their rating, now that they see what other items are available. It is important to note that the person who traded an item may give it a 3, while the one who received it may give it a 2. This does not mean that the trade was not beneficial.*

What is important is that people who receive an item give it a higher score than the score of the item they traded away.)

10. Tell the students that one more trading session will take place. This time they may trade with anyone in the class. They have five minutes to make any and all trades they wish to make. Again, no one is required to trade.

11. At the end of the five-minute trading session, call the students back to order. Ask them to display the items they now possess on their desks. Ask them to rate the item(s) on a scale of 1-5.

12. Conduct a debriefing discussion with the students, using the following questions:

A. How many of you made trades in Round 1? In Round 2? (Have a show of hands more people probably traded in Round 2 than in Round 1.)

B. Why did more trades take place in Round 2 than in Round 1? (More time to trade, better trading information existed as a result of Round 1, more alternative items were available to trade. Stress the idea that trade in Round 1 was similar to trading within a country, while trading in Round 2 was more like international trade. Note that the source of gains from trade are exactly the same in both rounds—i.e., in both intranational and international trade. In both rounds people traded things when they valued what they received more than what they gave up.)

C. What items were traded? *(Get some sample answers.)*

D. Which items were most popular, least popular? *(Get some sample answers.)*

E. Why did you trade? *(People tend to trade items they personally value less for items they value more.)*

F. What was the cost of your trade? *(The item given to the other person in the trade.)*

G. What was the benefit received from your trade? *(The item received from the other person in the exchange.)*

H. How many people rate the item they traded for higher than the item they had originally? *(Almost everyone who traded will rate the new item higher. This evidence should confirm the answers to Question E on Visual 1.)*

I. Did anyone make a mistake and trade badly? Did anyone fail to make a trade they now wish they had made? *(Often, someone will make a mistake. Not all trades turn out as expected, and not every trading opportunity is seized.)*

J. If students say they made a mistake, ask if they would make the same mistake next time. *(Maybe not. People tend to learn from their mistakes, and bad trades often lead people to stop making that trade or to stop trading with certain people or companies.)*

K. Which people had the most difficulty trading with others? *(People with unpopular items. To trade, you must have or produce items other people want.)*

L. Why did some people choose not to trade? *(People who preferred the items they had over the items offered to them had no incentive to trade.)*

13. Display Visual 2. Explain to the students that they must now draw some conclusions about trade in general. See if they agree with the definition of trade presented in Visual 2. Stress the *voluntary* nature of trade.

14. Display Visual 3. Ask the students if they agree with these statements about the motives for trade. Ask them for examples of their motives during the trading activity which are consistent with these statements.

15. Compare these explanations for why people trade with the students' initial statements in response to Visual 1. Revise the initial statements so they are consistent with the evidence from the activity and the statements in Visual 3.

16. Ask the students if they can identify examples of involuntary trade. (A mugging where a thief says, "Your money or your life." When you are ordered to cut the grass for a price set by your parents, or to pay income taxes or go to jail.) Ask students to discuss the question: Do these "trades" always increase satisfaction and wealth, or do they ever?

17. Summarize the main points of this lesson:

A. Trade is the voluntary exchange of goods and services.

B. People trade because they expect to gain from the trade.

ASSESSMENT
Provide the following information to students and ask them to respond to the question.

In 1994, Canadian businesses and individuals sold $195.8 billion of goods and services in the United States, while businesses and individuals in the United States sold $229.7 billion of goods and services in Canada. Why were these businesses and individuals trading with one another when they live in different countries?

(Suggested answer: They are trading because they gain from these exchanges. Otherwise they would not make these trades. Their national citizenship has little to do with their decision to trade.)

Why Do People Trade?

Trade Is the Voluntary Exchange of Goods and Services Among Individuals and Businesses.

Motive for Trading

People expect to gain by trading with other people. They hope to receive a good or service that is more valuable than whatever they trade away.

Motive for Not Trading

People do not trade when the good or service being offered is of less value than the good or service they are asked to exchange.

WHY PEOPLE AND NATIONS TRADE

INTRODUCTION

This lesson introduces the idea of comparative advantage as the basis for exchange between individuals and for international trade. Although many people believe that trade takes place so that people can get things that they couldn't produce themselves, the more basic reason for trade is the difference in relative costs of producing goods and services. In this lesson, students work through examples showing benefits from specializing according to comparative advantage. They discover how trade can make both trading partners better off, even though one party may initially appear to be better at producing everything.

CONCEPTS

International trade
Specialization
Comparative advantage
Gains from trade
Cost

CONTENT STANDARDS

Voluntary exchange occurs only when all participating parties expect to gain. This is true for trade among individuals or organizations within a nation, and among individuals or organizations in different nations.

Free trade increases worldwide material standards of living.

Voluntary exchange among people or organizations in different countries gives people a broader range of choices in buying goods and services.

When individuals, regions, and nations specialize in what they can produce at the lowest cost and then trade with others, both production and consumption levels increase.

Like trade among individuals within one country, international trade promotes specialization and division of labor and increases output and consumption.

OBJECTIVES

◆ Identify reasons for trade.
◆ Examine risks involved in specialization and free trade.
◆ Demonstrate the principle of comparative advantage.
◆ Apply the principle of comparative advantage to a hypothetical example of international trade.

LESSON DESCRIPTION

Students read and discuss a brief article on why nations trade, and they complete two activities applying the concept of comparative advantage. One activity involves exchange between two students; the second activity involves a hypothetical example of international trade.

TIME REQUIRED

One class period.

MATERIALS

★ One copy of Activities 1, 2, and 3 for each student.
★ Optional: One transparency of the chart on Activity 2.

PROCEDURE

1. Ask the students why people trade with each other. Encourage them to discuss trade between individuals as well as trade between countries. Write their answers on the board. (Note: If you have done Lesson 1 with the students, this step can be abbreviated or skipped.)

2. Distribute a copy of Activity 1, **Why People and Nations Trade**, to each student. Give students time to read the article.

3. Discuss Activity 1:

   A. Why do people trade for goods that they could produce themselves?

B. How do people gain from trade?

C. The United States is a large, wealthy country. Why would we want to trade with a small, poorer country such as Honduras? *(Make sure that students understand the principle of comparative advantage as explained in the activity. A country [or person] has the comparative advantage in producing a good if they produce it at a lower cost than their trading partner. Whoever can produce something at a lower cost should specialize in producing that good, and trade for goods that are more costly for them to produce. It is important to point out that because of scarcity and opportunity cost, no country [or person] can have a comparative advantage in producing everything. If you are very good in producing one thing, that makes producing something else more costly. Therefore, trade can benefit both large and small countries, and both rich and poor countries.)*

4. Distribute a copy of Activity 2 to each student. You may want each student to work with a partner. Ask students to complete the activity and to think about how it relates to the ideas of comparative advantage and trade. If some students have difficulty with the activity, let them talk with other students who can explain it to them. *(As demonstrated on this handout, thoroughly explaining the principle of comparative advantage involves using basic mathematics. Some students may get lost in the numbers, but many others find it very beneficial to work through the numerical examples. Decide how much to emphasize the computations with your students. For a class of predominantly low-achieving students, you may find it helpful to display a transparency of the chart on Activity 2 and work through it together as a class.)*

5. Go over the answers to Activity 2 with students. Point out that Sara and Rob are specializing according to their comparative advantage. That way, they actually trade their best relative skills with each other. The low-cost producer of a good or service has a comparative advantage in producing that good. Emphasize that even though Sara is better at writing captions and pasting pictures, it is still to her advantage to specialize in doing some work and to work with Rob for other work he does. Note that when Sara and Rob specialize according to their comparative advantage, they finish the job in as short a time as possible. Ask students to try to come up with a method that is better than Option 4. *(They will not be able to do this.)* Discuss how the ideas in this activity relate to comparative advantage in international trade.

6. Distribute a copy of Activity 3 to each student; allow time for them to read the introductory paragraphs. Ask the students to respond to the questions on the handout with a partner or in a small group. (If you wish, you may complete the handout with the class as a whole, discussing the answers as you go along.) *To make the computations easier, the numbers used in this handout are the same as the numbers in Activity 2. "Cheese" is equivalent to "captions" and "peanuts" are equivalent to "pictures." Optional: If students have studied opportunity cost before, you may wish to review this idea and point out that this is the cost concept used in this lesson.*

7. Go over the answers on Activity 3 with the class. Emphasize that through specialization and trade, people in *both* countries are able to consume more cheese and more peanuts than they could before they specialized and traded. This result occurs because the two countries have different costs of producing bread and cheese, which allows the principle of comparative advantage to work to everyone's benefit. Trade is a "win-win" situation, even though the Saratovians initially appear to be better at producing both cheese and peanuts.

ASSESSMENT

To evaluate students' understanding, ask them to explain in writing how the concept of comparative advantage would help people make an efficient economic choice in the following example:

Jennifer is a lawyer in great demand who earns $100 per hour. She is also an accomplished word processor who types errorless documents at 80 words per minute. Chris is a secretary who earns $8 per hour and types errorless documents at a rate of 40 words per minute. Both Jennifer and Chris work eight hours per day. Should Jennifer attempt to save money by firing Chris and doing all her own word processing?

(Jennifer should not do her own word processing. Her opportunity cost of typing is the $100 per hour she would earn as a lawyer. Although she could type in four hours the same amount that Chris could type in eight hours, it would cost Jennifer $400 in forgone income to type for herself. She could hire Chris for $64 per day; in typing for herself, therefore, Jennifer would suffer a net loss of $336. Chris has the comparative advantage in word processing, so she should do the typing. Jennifer has the comparative advantage in legal work, so she should concentrate on that.)

ACTIVITY 1
WHY PEOPLE AND NATIONS TRADE

The term "international trade" is somewhat misleading. It may sound as if international trade decisions are made by high-ranking government officials, but for the most part this is not true. International trade generally takes place between private citizens—consumers and producers who happen to live in different countries. Someone in New York who runs a clothing business may want to sell clothes in Canada. Or someone in California may decide to buy clothing made in Mexico. Decisions like these bring about international trade.

At first glance the answer to the question "Why do people trade?" may seem to be that people want things they cannot produce themselves. For people in some countries, this might involve trading for natural resources such as coal or oil, or for foods that would not grow in their climates. However, the idea of people trading just to obtain things that they cannot produce is only part of the story.

People in countries that engage in foreign trade often import goods that could be or already are made in their own countries. For example, steel and automobiles are imported into the United States, although we produce steel and automobiles ourselves. These imports compete with American-made products. So why trade for goods that we could produce ourselves?

A more complete answer to the question "Why trade?" is that international trade, like other voluntary exchanges, results because both the buyer and the seller expect to gain from it. They gain when they give up one thing and get a good or service in exchange for one that they value more. If they valued the good they gave up more than the good or service they received, they would not trade. In the same way, if importers and exporters in trading countries did not expect to be better off, trade would not take place. Americans decide to import Toyotas and bananas, and export Levis and machinery, because they expect to gain. The same goes for those in other countries who sell Toyotas and bananas to Americans and buy Levis and machinery from Americans.

Let's see how this works by looking at the example of American wheat and Honduran bananas. Most American wheat farmers could grow bananas in greenhouses, yet they prefer to buy imported bananas and continue to grow wheat instead. Why? The answer is obvious, but important. It would be relatively costly for American wheat farmers to grow bananas rather than wheat. To grow bananas they would have to buy and maintain greenhouses, as well as give up valuable land and time that they could use to grow wheat. They would be better off if they concentrated on producing wheat instead. Their land and climate are better suited to growing wheat, and they already have the necessary equipment.

Does this mean that American wheat farmers must go without bananas? The answer is an obvious "no." They trade wheat for dollars and use dollars to buy bananas grown in Honduras, in a climate better suited for banana growing. The Hondurans who sell bananas can use the money they earn from selling bananas to purchase things that would be more costly to produce themselves.

When people specialize in the production of less costly goods, and trade for goods that are more costly to produce, they are following the principle of comparative advantage. Comparative advantage means having a cost advantage in the production of one type of good or service compared to the production of some other good or service. Both trading partners can gain if they specialize in the production of things that they produce at the lowest cost.

Despite the advantages of following the principle of comparative advantage. specialization does have risks. In general, when people specialize they depend on trading partners for other goods and services that they want. Some of the specific risks involved are:

1. Will other products you wish to buy be available by trading? For example. what if your business depends on imported sugar, and this sugar becomes unavailable because of political problems?

2. Will people and businesses in other countries be willing to purchase the products produced in our specialized economy? What if another country sets up trade restrictions so that people cannot buy U.S. exports?

3. Do people in a given country want to be dependent on foreigners for vital goods, such as food, energy, or medicine? This could happen for people who do not have the comparative advantage in producing these goods and specialize in producing other goods to trade.

The answers to these and related questions influence whether countries establish laws that limit free trade.

What about you? Do you engage in international trade? Every time you buy a product made in a foreign country, you send a message to importers in this country and exporters in other countries. You say that you think you can gain by buying certain types of products produced in other countries. Let's say that you own shoes made in China. Why didn't you make your own shoes, or why didn't you buy American-made shoes instead? Your decision to trade your money for foreign-made goods illustrates how the concept of comparative advantage is important to the economic choices you make every day.

ACTIVITY 2
COMPARATIVE ADVANTAGE

Rob and Sara, editors of the Central High School yearbook, have a big problem. It is Monday after school, and they have just discovered that six pages of the yearbook sports section somehow got mixed up with the Ecology Club's recycling project. The yearbook pages have been shredded at the local ecology center. To make matters worse, the rest of the yearbook staff left school before the crisis was discovered. The yearbook advisor is insisting that Rob and Sara stay after school to re-do the pages to meet Tuesday's deadline. Neither is to leave before all six pages are finished. Both Rob and Sara want to finish in as short a time as possible.

Each of the six missing pages has to include five pictures, with a caption below each picture. Luckily, there are sports pictures available to replace the ones that have been recycled, but the pictures must be cropped and pasted on layout pages. Sara figures it takes her about one minute to crop and paste a picture, and about two minutes to write a good caption. Rob, on the other hand, takes about two minutes to crop and paste a picture, and about five minutes to write a good caption.

	Sara	Rob
Time to crop and paste one picture		
Time to write 1 caption		
Time to finish 1 page (5 pictures and 5 captions)		
Time to finish 3 pages		
Time to finish all pictures (6 pages with 5 pictures on each page)		
Time to finish all captions (6 pages with 5 captions on each page)		
Time to finish all 6 pages		

1. Use the information above to fill in the table. (Assume that the tasks may be done simultaneously — i.e., that Rob and Sara do not have to paste a picture first, and then write a caption.)

2. Analyze the options below to determine how Rob and Sara could finish the job in the shortest possible time.

Option 1: Rob suggests that Sara do all the pages. He says it is clear that she is better at both writing the captions and doing the pictures. If he tries to help, he might just get in her way and slow her down.

Option 2: The yearbook advisor suggests that Rob and Sara divide up the pages, with each completing 3 pages. She thinks that this would be the fairest way, since each would do half the work.

Option 3: After listening to the yearbook advisor and to Rob, Sara suggests combining their ideas. She offers to do four pages, and Rob can do two pages. This way she won't be doing all the work while Rob does nothing. Since Sara recognizes that she can complete both pictures and captions faster than Rob, she is willing to do more pages than Rob to save time.

ACTIVITY 2 (continued)

Option 4: Rob's friend Kira, who is studying economics, has been listening to the conversation. Kira says that Sara has the comparative advantage in writing the captions. This is because in the time it takes Sara to write one caption, she gives up finishing only two pictures, whereas for every caption Rob writes he gives up finishing two and a half pictures. Rob has the comparative advantage in finishing pictures. In the time it takes him to finish one picture, he gives up finishing only 2/5 (40%) of a caption. In the time it takes Sara to finish one picture, she gives up finishing 1/2 (50%) of a caption. Kira says that the most efficient way to complete the yearbook pages is to have each person specialize where he or she has the comparative advantage, so Sara should do all the captions and Rob should do all the pictures.

Assume that it is now 3:30 p.m. Remember that neither Rob nor Sara can leave school until the entire job is finished. In other words, if Sara finishes her part at 4:00 and Rob finishes his part at 6:00, they both must stay until Rob finishes at 6:00.

1. By what time could Rob and Sara finish the job and leave school if they chose:

Option 1?_____.

Option 2?_____.

Option 3?_____.

Option 4?_____.

2. Which option allows them to complete the task in the shortest period of time?_____.

ACTIVITY 2 (continued)
ANSWER KEY FOR TEACHERS

1.

	Sara	Rob
Time to crop and paste one picture	1 minute	2 minutes
Time to write 1 caption	2 minutes	5 minutes
Time to finish 1 page (5 pictures and 5 captions)	15 minutes	35 minutes
Time to finish 3 pages	45 minutes	105 minutes (1 hour 45 minutes)
Time to finish all pictures (6 pages with 5 pictures on each page)	30 minutes	60 minutes
Time to finish all captions (6 pages with 5 captions on each page)	60 minutes	150 minutes (2 1/2 hours)
Time to finish all 6 pages	90 minutes (1-1/2 hours)	210 minutes (3-1/2 hours)

Option 1: Sara does all the pages.

Option 2: Rob and Sara divide up the pages, with each completing 3 pages.

Option 3: Sara does 4 pages, Rob does 2 pages.

Option 4: Sara does all the captions, Rob does all the pictures.1.

Assume that it is now 3:30 p.m. Remember that neither Rob nor Sara can leave school until the job is finished. In other words, if Sara finishes her part at 4:00 and Rob finishes his at 6:00, they both must stay until Rob finishes at 6:00.

1. By what time could Rob and Sara finish the job and leave school if they choose:

Option 1? *If Sara does all the pages, they may leave in 90 minutes, at 5 p.m.*

Option 2? *If Rob and Sara each do 3 pages, they will finish in 105 minutes (1 hour and 45 minutes), when Rob finishes his pages. They could leave at 5:15 p.m.*

Option 3? *Sara would finish her 4 pages in 60 minutes, and Rob would finish his 2 pages in 70 minutes (1 hour and 10 minutes). They could leave at 4:40 p.m.*

Option 4? *It would take Sara 1 hour to finish the captions, and Rob 1 hour to finish the pictures. They could leave at 4:30 p.m.*

2. Which option allows them to complete the task in the shortest period of time? *Option 4.*

ACTIVITY 3
COMPARATIVE ADVANTAGE AND INTERNATIONAL TRADE

Comparative advantage is a very important concept in economics because it provides the basis for trade between individuals, for trade within a country, and for international trade. When countries specialize in producing those goods that they can make at a lower cost than their trading partners can, total output will be larger than without specialization. If the countries then trade with each other, they are able to consume more than if they were self-sufficient and didn't trade. In Activity 2, you worked through a problem where Sara and Rob specialized according to their comparative advantage to finish yearbook pages. Use the same concepts now to see how specializing according to comparative advantage can make countries better off.

Instead of Sara and Rob, assume that we are looking at two countries, Saratovia and Robland. Like all countries, Saratovia and Robland have limited resources to use in producing goods and services. People in both countries have decided to use their resources to produce two goods: peanuts and cheese. Assume that a Saratovian, working for one day, can produce either 60 pounds of peanuts or 30 pounds of cheese. A Roblander, working for one day, can produce either 30 pounds of peanuts or 12 pounds of cheese.

1. COST

Economists think of cost as what is given up when one good is produced instead of another. For example, if people in Robland produce 30 pounds of peanuts, they give up producing 12 pounds of cheese. So in Robland the cost of 30 pounds of peanuts is 12 pounds of cheese.

Since the cost of 12 pounds of cheese = 30 pounds of peanuts in Robland, to find the cost of 1 pound of cheese divide both 12 and 30 by 12. Therefore, in Robland the cost of 1 pound of cheese = $2^1/_2$ pounds of peanuts.

Since the cost of 12 pounds of cheese = 30 pounds of peanuts in Robland, to find the cost of 1 pound of peanuts divide both 12 and 30 by 30. Therefore, in Robland the cost of 1 pound of peanuts is 2/5 (40%) of a pound of cheese.

Now you calculate the cost of cheese and peanuts in Saratovia:

The cost of 30 pounds of cheese in Saratovia is _____ pounds of peanuts.

The cost of 1 pound of cheese in Saratovia is _____ pounds of peanuts.

The cost of 1 pound of peanuts in Saratovia is _____ pounds of cheese.

2. COMPARATIVE ADVANTAGE

Peanuts can be produced at a lower cost in _____, and cheese can be produced at a lower cost in _____.

Therefore, Saratovia has the comparative advantage in producing _____, and Robland has the comparative advantage in producing _____.

3. WITHOUT SPECIALIZATION

Suppose that during one day 100 Saratovians can decide to produce any of the following combinations of cheese and peanuts (in pounds). They are currently producing the combination shown in the boxes, 2000 pounds of cheese and 2000 pounds of peanuts:

ACTIVITY 3 (continued)

CHEESE	PEANUTS
3000	0
2000	2000
1000	4000
0	6000

During one day, 100 Roblanders can decide to produce any of the following combinations of cheese and peanuts (in pounds). They currently produce the combination shown in boxes, 900 pounds of cheese and 750 pounds of peanuts:

CHEESE	PEANUTS
1200	0
900	750
600	1500
360	2250
0	3000

At current production levels in the two countries, the total output for the two countries would be _____ pounds of cheese and _____ pounds of peanuts. However, both countries would like to have more cheese and more peanuts.

4. WITH SPECIALIZATION

Suppose all 100 Saratovian workers decided to produce only cheese. Suppose all 100 Roblanders decided to produce only peanuts. Use the information from #3 to complete these statements:

With specialization, the total output for the two countries from 100 workers is _____ pounds of cheese and _____ pounds of peanuts. This is a gain of _____ pounds of cheese and _____ pounds of peanuts, compared to #3.

5. TRADE

Assume that Saratovia is producing only cheese and Robland is producing only peanuts (as in #4), but they decide to trade, so that they will each have both cheese and peanuts. Saratovia trades 950 pounds of cheese to Robland in exchange for 2150 pounds of peanuts. After this trade, Saratovia has _____ pounds of cheese and _____ pounds of peanuts. Robland has _____ pounds of cheese and _____ pounds of peanuts. Are both countries better off than they were in question #3, before they specialized and traded?

ACTIVITY 3
ANSWER KEY FOR TEACHERS

1. COST

The cost of 30 pounds of cheese in Saratovia is _60_ pounds of peanuts.

The cost of 1 pound of cheese in Saratovia is _2_ pounds of peanuts.

The cost of 1 pound of peanuts in Saratovia is _1/2_ pounds of cheese.

2. COMPARATIVE ADVANTAGE

Peanuts can be produced at a lower cost in _Robland (since 2/5 is less than 1/2)_ and cheese can be produced at a lower cost in _Saratovia (since 2 is less than 2 1/2)._

Therefore, Saratovia has the comparative advantage in producing _cheese_, and Robland has the comparative advantage in producing _peanuts_.

3. WITHOUT SPECIALIZATION

The total output for the two countries would be _2900_ pounds of cheese and _2750_ pounds of _peanuts_.

4. WITH SPECIALIZATION

With specialization, the total output for the two countries is _3000_ pounds of cheese and _3000_ pounds of peanuts. This is a gain of _100_ pounds of cheese and _250_ pounds of peanuts, compared to #3.

5. TRADE

Saratovia trades 950 pounds of cheese to Robland in exchange for 2150 pounds of peanuts. After this trade, Saratovia has _2050_ pounds of cheese and _2150_ pounds of peanuts. Robland has _950_ pounds of cheese and _850_ pounds of peanuts. Both countries are better off than they were in question #3, before they specialized and traded. _They both have more cheese and more peanuts to consume._

TRADE AND SPECIALIZATION

INTRODUCTION

Living standards improve when people specialize and produce those items they can make most efficiently (at the lowest cost), and trade for other items that are more costly for them to produce. In this lesson students participate in a classroom simulation to learn how economic welfare is increased by trade and specialization. To explain this outcome, they apply the principle of comparative advantage to their trading activity.

CONCEPTS

Comparative advantage
Specialization
Trade

CONTENT STANDARDS

When individuals, regions, and nations specialize in what they can produce at the lowest cost and then trade with others, both production and consumption increase.

Economic specialization occurs when people concentrate their production on fewer kinds of goods and services than they consume.

Division of labor occurs when the production of a good is broken down into numerous separate tasks, with different workers performing each task.

Specialization and division of labor usually increase the productivity of workers.

As a result of growing international economic interdependence, economic conditions and policies in one nation increasingly affect economic conditions and policies in other nations.

OBJECTIVES

◆ Identify examples of trading activity in a classroom simulation.
◆ Explain how trading in a classroom simulation is similar to and different from "real-world" examples of trading.
◆ Explain how living standards improve as a result of trade and specialization.

LESSON DESCRIPTION

In this lesson students learn by participating in a classroom simulation how economic welfare is increased by trade and specialization. To explain this outcome they must apply the principle of comparative advantage to their trading activity. Students pick particular professions, trade with one another in a series of trading rounds, and discover that living standards improve when people specialize in producing what they produce most efficiently and trade for other things they want.

TIME REQUIRED

One class period.

MATERIALS

★ One copy of Activity 1 for each student
★ One copy of Activity 2 for each student for each of three trading rounds
★ Several small prizes (optional)

PROCEDURE

1. Divide the class into thirds. Designate one group as farmers, one group as tailors, and one group as builders.

2. Distribute one copy of Activity 1 and 2 to each student. Ask the students to write their role assignments (farmer, tailor, or builder) in the first blank. In the second blank, have the farmers write "food," the tailors write "clothing," and the builders write "shelter." Ask the students to read the instructions; tell them each round will last exactly three minutes. Have students enter production figures for the round (600 units of their specialty or 100 units of all three goods).

3. **Round 1.** Let students walk around the classroom to conduct their trades. End the round after three minutes, and have the students return to their seats. Tell them to subtract 100 from each column to account for basic necessities. Any student with a negative number in any column "dies" and is out of the

game. Ask who has the highest net gain. You may wish to award a small prize to this student.

4. **Round 2.** Have the students enter new production figures for this round (600 units of their specialty or 100 units each of all three goods). Conduct Round 2 in the same manner as Round 1.

5. **Round 3 (Final Round).** Conduct the round as before. Have the students tally their net gains from all three rounds. The student with the highest overall net gain is the classroom winner. (*Optional*: Award a "grand prize.")

6. Explain that the calculation of net gain is based on the assumption that the value of one unit of each of the goods is equal across all three goods and for all individuals.

7. Ask the students how they were able to achieve a standard of living higher than the bare minimum needed for survival. (*Answer: By specialization and trade.*) Ask if any students chose not to specialize. Why might a person not specialize? (*Answer: To avoid dependence on others.*)

8. Explain to the class that the game they played illustrates the concept of comparative advantage. Comparative advantage exists when one person (or firm or region or nation) can produce a product at a lower opportunity cost compared to other products. Opportunity cost refers to what is given up to do something else. Therefore, farmers had higher costs of producing clothing and shelter, but lower costs of producing food. Tailors had higher costs of producing food and shelter, but lower costs of producing clothing. Builders had lower costs of producing food and clothing, but lower costs of producing shelter.

9. Now conduct a more sophisticated example of this exercise. Divide the class in half and designate one group as skilled workers and the other group as unskilled workers. Tell the skilled workers that they can produce any one

of the following three sets of products in one round: (a) 400 units of food, or (b) 400 units of shelter, or (c) 100 units of food and 300 units of shelter. Tell the unskilled workers they can produce any one of the following three sets in one round: (a) 300 units of food, or (b) 100 units of shelter, or (c) 75 units of food and 75 units of shelter. Explain to the class that in this situation the skilled workers have an absolute advantage in production of both food and shelter. Ask the class: is there any reason why a skilled worker would want to engage in trade with an unskilled worker under these conditions? (*The answer is yes, but don't indicate this immediately. You are likely to get a variety of responses from students.*) Tell the class that you are going to conduct some experiments to see if the answer can be determined.

A. Have all workers produce set (3), the mix of food and shelter. Determine the total number of units of food produced in the class by multiplying the number of skilled workers by 100 and the number of unskilled workers by 75, and adding up the results. Determine the total number of units of shelter produced in the class by the multiplying number of skilled workers by 300 and the number of unskilled workers by 75, and adding up the results. Explain that this is the total production of food and shelter in the economy without specialization and trade. (*You can either relax the assumption that 100 units of each good are required for survival, or point out that under this system unskilled workers will be in serious trouble.*)

B. Now introduce specialization by asking all skilled workers to produce shelter and all unskilled workers to produce food. Add up the total production in the economy. There should be much *more* total production than before.

C. Have all skilled workers produce food and all unskilled workers produce shelter. There should now be much *less* total production than before. Explain to the class that for specialization and trade to increase output, people should specialize by producing the product in which they have a comparative advantage. Skilled workers have to give up less food to produce shelter than unskilled workers, so they have the comparative advantage in producing shelter. But unskilled workers have to give up less shelter to produce foods, so they have the comparative advantage in producing food. Specializing according to comparative advantage increases production levels and, therefore, the quantity of goods and services that are available for consumption.

D. Show students how to calculate comparative advantages. In this exercise the opportunity cost of one unit of food to the skilled worker was one unit of shelter (producing set [c] instead of set [b] entails giving up 100 units of shelter to get 100 units of food), but to the unskilled worker the opportunity cost of one unit of food was only one-third unit of shelter (producing set [c] instead of set [b] entails giving up 25 units of shelter to get 75 units of food). Conversely, the opportunity cost of one unit of shelter to the skilled worker was one unit of food, but to the unskilled worker the opportunity cost was three units of food. Thus, the skilled worker has a comparative advantage in building and the unskilled worker a comparative advantage in food production.

ASSESSMENT

Evaluate student answers to the questions in the procedure section. In addition, the following questions might be asked:

1. Can you think of examples of comparative advantage between regions of the United States? Between countries of the world?

2. True or False? When people, regions, or nations specialize and trade, there must be a winner and there must be a loser. *(False. Trade only takes place if both parties expect to gain, and the standard of living of both parties can increase because total production levels are increased through specialization and trade.)*

3. Explain comparative advantage. *(A comparative advantage exists for a producer if the opportunity cost of producing a good is lower than the opportunity cost other producers face in producing that product.)*

4. Jennifer and her younger brother Tom have been told by their parents to mow the lawn and wash the car. There is enough equipment for them to work together on each task. Should they do so? Jennifer can mow the lawn in one hour and wash the car in a quarter of an hour. Tom can mow the lawn in two hours and wash the car in one hour. What is Jennifer's comparative advantage? *(Washing the car, since her opportunity cost of washing the car is 1/4 lawn mowed, while it costs Tom more (1/2 lawn mowed) to wash the car. Conversely, Tom has a comparative advantage in lawn mowing, since when he mows the lawn he gives up washing 2 cars while Jennifer gives up washing 4 cars.)* How would you recommend they divide the work and complete the tasks in the least possible time? *(Jennifer should wash the car alone and help her brother Tom finish the mowing.)*

ACTIVITY 1
TRADING RECORDS

You are a skilled _____. You may spend your time in each round to produce 600 units of _____, or instead you may produce 100 units each of food, shelter, and clothing. You must choose what you will produce at the beginning of each round.

Your basic survival needs are 100 units each of food, clothing, and shelter during each round. If you do not acquire a minimum of 100 units of each of these items, you will die. If you use all your time to produce each of these items for yourself, you will be able to produce enough to meet your basic needs, but you will having nothing left over. As an alternative, you can spend your time working to produce what you produce best, and then you can trade this production for whatever else you need. Any extra production above what is needed to survive raises your standard of living.

The objective of the game is to achieve the highest standard of living. Use the trading record in Activity 2 to record your initial production on line 1 and your trades on subsequent lines. *Example:* If you are a farmer and decide to produce 600 units of food, write 600 under the food column on line 1. Let's say you then trade 100 units of food with Andrea for 100 units of shelter. On line 2 subtract 100 from your food column and add 100 to your shelter column. Let's say you then trade 150 units of food for 100 units of clothing with Tim. To show this, you will subtract 150 from your food column and add 100 to your clothing column. At the conclusion of each round, subtract 100 from each column to represent your basic survival needs. Any units remaining after that add to your standard of living.

If any column is negative at the end of any round, you are "dead" and out of the game. If you are still in the game, determine your net gain for the round by adding your net gains for food, clothing, and shelter (line 5). The person with the highest numerical net gain achieves the highest standard of living and wins the round.

Example of Trading Exchange Record

Transaction	Food	Shelter	Clothing	Net Gain
1. Initial production	600			
2. Trade with Andrea	-100	100		
	500			
3. Trade with Tim	-150		100	
	350			
4. End-of-round basic needs	-100	-100	-100	
	250	0	0	250
5. Net gain				

ACTIVITY 2
TRADING RECORD

Transaction	Food	Shelter	Clothing	Net Gain
1. _____	_____	_____	_____	_____
2. _____	_____	_____	_____	_____
3. _____	_____	_____	_____	_____
4. _____	_____	_____	_____	_____
5. _____	_____	_____	_____	_____
6. _____	_____	_____	_____	_____
7. _____	_____	_____	_____	_____
8. _____	_____	_____	_____	_____
9. _____	_____	_____	_____	_____
10. _____	_____	_____	_____	_____
11. _____	_____	_____	_____	_____
12. _____	_____	_____	_____	_____
13. _____	_____	_____	_____	_____
14. _____	_____	_____	_____	_____
15. _____	_____	_____	_____	_____

TRADING AROUND THE WORLD

INTRODUCTION

Students often do not appreciate how pervasive international trade is and how much it is growing. For example, in 1959 exports accounted for only 4 percent of U.S. GNP. By 1995, that had nearly tripled. Economists expect this growth to continue, and each year more and more large and small businesses rely on international markets for their success, or compete with imported products that U.S. consumers are obviously more and more willing to buy. In all of these ways, international trade has a large and growing impact on students' lives.

Two key factors in the increase in world trade have been improved communications and transportation technology. Information today travels all over the world at the speed of light, and jumbo jets and huge supertankers crisscross the globe loaded with new and improved products. You hear it said many times, but it really is true that we live in an increasingly global economy.

CONCEPTS

Trade
Specialization
Interdependence
Free trade
Trade barriers

CONTENT STANDARD

When individuals, regions, and nations specialize in what they can produce at the lowest cost and then trade with others, both production and consumption increase.

Two factors that prompt international trade are international differences in the availability of productive resources and differences in relative prices.

Individuals and nations have a comparative advantage in the production of goods or services if they can produce at a lower opportunity cost than other individuals or nations.

As a result of growing international economic interdependence, economic conditions and policies in one nation increasingly affect economic conditions and policies in other nations.

OBJECTIVES

◆ Explain that international trade among nations has increased in recent decades and continues to increase.
◆ Understand several ways in which international trade affects everyday life.
◆ Identify the major countries that purchase U.S. exports.
◆ Identify the major countries that sell imports to people in the United States.

LESSON DESCRIPTION

Students first analyze and discuss information on the major U.S. trading partners. Then they identify the parent countries of businesses that produce familiar brand name products. Finally, students participate in an activity to identify the countries where clothing and other items seen in their classroom were produced.

TIME REQUIRED

One class period.

MATERIALS

★ One transparency each of Visuals 1, 2, and 3
★ One copy of Activity 1 for each student
★ Water-based transparency markers

PROCEDURE

1. Explain to the students that international trade has increased greatly throughout the world. Discuss the basic reasons why this has occurred. *(Improvements in communication and transportation technology. Lowering of trade barriers through treaties such as NAFTA and WTO. Increased income levels lead to increased demand for imported goods in many countries.)*

2. Discuss the terms "exports" and "imports." Ask the students to guess what percent of our GDP is imports. (*15.7%*) What percent of our GDP do we export? (*13.5%*) Ask the students to guess the top three nations that purchase U. S. exports, and the top three suppliers of U.S. imports. (*Discuss Visual 1*)

3. To explore how interdependent world business has become, and how many companies that produce familiar brand name products are actually foreign owned, display Visual 2, **Where In the World?** Ask the students to identify the home country of the listed products. Ask how foreign countries could produce so many common U.S. products. (*Many products were first produced by U.S. firms, which were subsequently bought by foreign owners. Similarly, U.S. firms often buy foreign companies and market their products abroad.*)

ANSWERS TO VISUAL 2, WHERE IN THE WORLD?

Nestle - Switzerland	Vaseline - Great Britain
Volvo - Sweden	Friskies - Switzerland
Shell - Netherlands	Bayer Aspirin - Germany
Sony - Japan	Nike - United States
Lipton Tea - Great Britain	Gatorade - United States
Baskin-Robbins - Great Britain	Hardee's - Canada
Tropicana - Canada	Adidas - Germany
Burger King - Great Britain	Levi Strauss - United States
TV Guide - Australia	Alka-Seltzer - Germany
Firestone - Japan	Michelin Tires - France
CBS Television - United States	Fila Shoes - Italy
Ragu - Great Britain	Bumble Bee Tuna - Thailand

---

4. **The Label Search Activity**

A. Divide students into groups of five. Give each group the following:

- one copy of Activity 1, **The Label Search**, for each student

- one transparency of Visual 3, **World Map**, for each team

- one water-based marker for each team (perhaps using different colors for different teams)

B. Each student will search the room for at least five clothing items and other items produced in another country. Allow students about 5-10 minutes for the search, and have the students record their findings on scrap paper. Students must identify the specific item (e.g., John's coat) and the country where it was produced.

C. In their groups, the students should compile their data and list at least 10 different items on Activity 1. Then the groups should color the countries where these products were made on the transparency of the world map.

D. The groups should then answer the remaining questions on Activity 1. (You may choose to have each student complete a copy of this handout.)

E. Have one group member explain the group's findings on the overhead. Have the class identify patterns on each group's transparency. *(Possible patterns: many products from Asia; none or few from Africa or the former Soviet Union; certain types of products come from certain countries or regions, etc. Discuss why these patterns occur.)*

F. Discuss the answers to the other questions on Activity 1.

Possible Answers for Activity 1:

A. *Geography and climate greatly influence what a country produces. For example, a sweater may come from Scotland because Scotland's relatively mild climate and hilly land are good for raising sheep. However, students may discover that sweaters are often made in countries not noted for wool production, such as Taiwan or South Korea. This is because low-cost labor, not natural resources, provides the greatest production advantage. These countries can purchase wool from other countries that specialize in wool production (such as Scotland) and then manufacture the sweaters. Because of modern communication and transportation technology, countries today are less constrained in their production by the natural resources available in their physical geography.*

B. *Some patterns will emerge. No goods at all may come from certain geographic areas (Africa, former Soviet Union, etc.). Electronic equipment may come mostly from Asian countries; shoes mostly from Italy, Brazil, Korea, or China. Students will also discover that many goods are produced in the U.S.*

C. *When two parties trade, both expect to benefit. Each exchanges something valued less for something valued more.*

D. *More.*

E. *Answers will vary. Being more dependent is helpful in that consumers have access to more and better goods and services at lower prices. Increased interdependence through trade may lessen the chance for disputes turning into wars. There are possible disadvantages, however. When a country is dependent on others it may find itself without key resources if wars do occur. Or a country may be faced with sudden price increases in key products, such as oil, as a result of changes in trading patterns or political policies in other countries.*

F. *Groups' views will vary, but most economists are strong supporters of free trade and oppose trade barriers because trade increases income, output, and consumption levels globally.*

ASSESSMENT

Ask the students what new insights they gained by doing this lesson. Discuss any disagreements there may have been in answering the questions on Activity 1. Assign the students to write paragraphs that complete the following statements:

A. *In this lesson I learned that....*

B. *International trade is beneficial to me because....*

VISUAL 1
WHERE IN THE WORLD?

Top 10 Purchasers of U.S. Exports—1995

Country	Billions of Dollars	Percent of Total Exports
Canada	127.2	21.8
Japan	64.3	11.0
Mexico	46.3	7.9
United Kingdom	28.8	4.9
South Korea	25.4	4.3
Germany	22.4	3.8
Taiwan	19.3	3.2
Netherlands	16.5	2.8
Singapore	15.3	2.6
France	14.2	2.4

Total Exports from the U.S.   **$647.6 Billion**

Source: Statistical Abstract of the United States—1996

Top 10 Suppliers of U.S. Imports—1995

Country	Billions of Dollars	Percent of Total Imports
Canada	145.3	19.6
Japan	123.5	16.6
Mexico	49.5	6.7
China	45.5	6.1
Germany	36.8	5.0
Taiwan	29.0	3.9
United Kingdom	26.9	3.6
South Korea	24.2	3.3
Singapore	18.6	2.5
Malaysia	17.5	2.3

Total Imports into the U.S.   **$743.3 Billion**

Source: Statistical; Abstract of the United States—1996

VISUAL 2
WHERE IN THE WORLD?

What are the home countries of the firms that produce these products?

Nestle _____

Shell _____

Lipton Tea _____

Baskin-Robbins _____

Burger King _____

Firestone _____

Ragu _____

Friskies _____

Nike _____

Hardee's _____

Levi Strauss _____

Michelin Tires _____

Bumble Bee Tuna _____

Volvo _____

Sony _____

Tropicana _____

TV Guide _____

CBS Television _____

Vaseline _____

Bayer Aspirin _____

Gatorade _____

Adidas _____

Alka-Seltzer _____

Fila Shoes _____

VISUAL 3
WORLD MAP

From *Focus: International Economics*, © National Council on Economic Education, New York, NY.

ACTIVITY 1
LABEL SEARCH

Group Members_____

1. Search the room for clothing and other items that were produced in other countries. Each member of your group must take part in the search. Find at least five items. On scrap paper write the name of the item (e.g., John's coat) and the country where it was produced.

2. Meet as a group and list at least ten different items and the countries where they were produced in the blanks below.

3. Color these countries on the World Map transparency.

4. Answer the rest of the questions on this handout.

A. Analyze your list carefully. What are some specific reasons why these countries specialize in the production of these items?

B. What patterns do you notice in where the items were produced?

Search Results	
Clothing or Item Description	**Country Where Produced**
1.	
2.	
3.	
4.	
5.	
6.	
7.	
8.	
9.	
10.	

C. When you or someone else buys the clothing or items produced in a foreign country, who benefits? Explain your answer.

D. Do you think trade makes our country more or less dependent on other countries for the things we want?

E. Do you think it is good or bad to be dependent on other countries for the things we buy? Explain your answer.

F. Discuss this statement. "To save American textile jobs, Congress should limit the number of foreign clothes that are imported into our country." Present your group's views to the class.

INTERPRETING TRADE DATA: GRAPHS AND CHARTS

INTRODUCTION

International trade contributes to global interdependence and represents an increasingly large part of the U.S. economy. For students to fully appreciate the impact trade has on their lives, they should learn to summarize and find patterns in economic data. Graphical analysis is a useful and convenient method of summarizing data. This lesson introduces students to the uses and possible misuses of graphs in interpreting economic data. The data presented here are readily available in many libraries should you want to update tables, using the sources indicated for each graph.

CONCEPTS

Exports
Imports
Real gross domestic product

CONTENT STANDARDS

When individuals, regions, and nations specialize in what they can produce at the lowest cost and then trade with others, both production and consumption increase.

Like trade among individuals within one country, international trade promotes specialization and division of labor and increases output and consumption.

As a result of growing international economic interdependence, economic conditions and policies in one nation increasingly affect economic conditions and policies in other nations.

OBJECTIVES

◆ Interpret graphs and charts.
◆ Draw inferences from economic data about the importance of trade to the United States.

LESSON DESCRIPTION

In this lesson students are given short readings and asked to interpret graphs displaying information about international trade. The twofold purpose is to learn how to read graphs and to understand the breadth and scope of world trade.

TIME REQUIRED

One class period.

MATERIALS

★ One copy of Activity 1, Part A, for each student
★ One copy of Activity 1, Part B, for each student
★ One copy of Activity 1, Part C, for each student

PROCEDURES

1. Distribute copies of Activity 1, Part A. Ask the students to read the instructions.

2. Ask the students to offer an interpretation of Figure 1 by writing one or two sentences summarizing the graphs.

3. Choose a few students to read their summary statements aloud.

4. Ask why there is so much difference in the summary statements. (Possible answers: a. There is too much information to summarize in one or two sentences. That is why we use graphs to summarize vast amounts of information. b. Students may not agree on the facts presented. c. Students may not agree on the interpretation of the facts.)

5. Refer students to Figures 1 and 2, and ask them to answer the following questions:

A. What is meant by "Billions of 1992 dollars?" (The data have been corrected for the effects of inflation by measuring every year's exports and imports with the same value of a dollar, holding all prices constant at 1992 levels. In other words, real GDP [Figure 4] is calculated by multiply-

ing production levels of final goods and services times their 1992 prices.)

B. What is the basic trend of exports since 1960? Of imports? *(Both have increased.)*

C. Why do you think exports and imports have risen? *(This is a very open-ended question; answers may include higher levels of real output in the U.S. and globally, plus a more integrated world economy, owing to improved communication and transportation technologies. Note that the effect of inflation has been removed by using 1992 prices in all years.)*

D. Do the graphs tell us why exports and imports seem to move together? *(No, but basically the reason people are willing to sell goods and services to people in other countries [export] is that they want to buy goods and services from the other countries [import]. I.e., exports generally pay for imports, so they tend to rise or fall together.)*

6. Have the students answer Questions 1-4 on Activity 1, Part B. (See the answer key at the end of the lesson.)

7. Referring to Activity 1, Figures 3 and 4, ask the students whether one can infer from the graphs that trade has grown in importance to the U.S. economy. *(No. Both graphs show absolute amounts, but the question asks for a relative measure.)*

8. Read students the following statement: "To help you understand the difference between absolute and relative measures, you will be constructing another graph from data provided in Activity 1, Part C. Notice that total trade and GDP are given in dollars; this is the same information that was plotted in the last graphs and is an absolute measure. But we could not infer from these graphs whether trade was growing or declining as a part of the U.S. economy. That requires a relative measure of the importance of

trade. To construct such a measure, divide total trade by the corresponding value of GDP for each year and multiply this result by 100. Enter the value in the table in the column labeled "Percentage." The first entry is completed for you.

9. Have the students plot this information on the graph in Figure 5.

10. Ask the students to write a summary of the information on the graph. *(Each summary should note that foreign trade as a percentage of GDP has increased in recent years, except for 1982.)*

ASSESSMENT

Assess the quality of student answers to discussion questions and the written summary of information in Figure 5.

ACTIVITY 1
PART A

PART A

A great deal of information is available about international trade. Most of this information is published in long tables of numbers which can overwhelm even economists and accountants. To reduce the problem of information overload, students should develop the skills of creating and interpreting graphical summaries. Consider the four graphs in this Activity. To communicate the same information in words would take considerable time and effort. Follow the instructions from your teacher and write a few brief sentences describing each of the following graphs.

U.S. Exports and Imports Since 1960 in Billions of 1992 dollars.

Figure 1 Exports

Billions of 1992 dollars

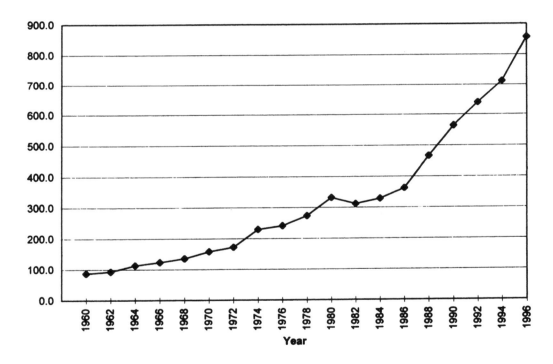

Source: *Economic Report of President, Table B-2, February 1998*

ACTIVITY 1, Part A (continued)

Figure 2 Imports

Billions of 1992 dollars

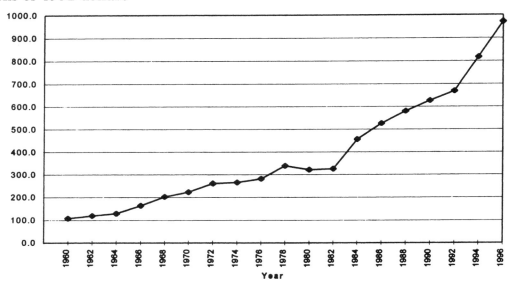

Figure 3 Total U.S. Trade: Exports plus Imports

Billions of 1992 dollars

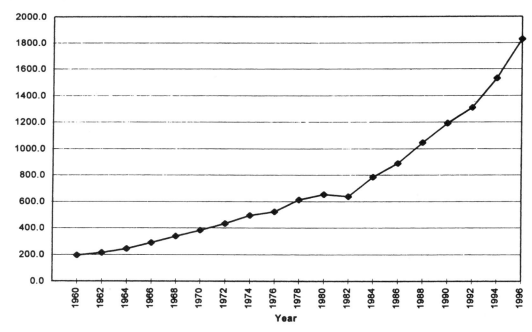

Source: *Economic Report of President*, Table B-2, February 1998.

ACTIVITY 1, PART A (continued)

Figure 4 National Output: Gross Domestic Product

Billions of 1992 dollars

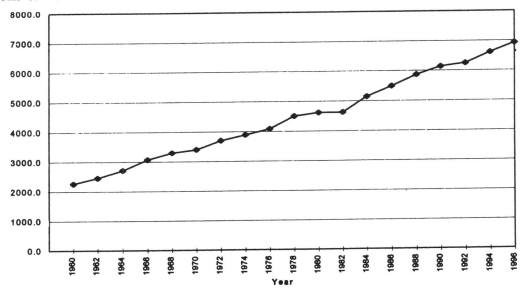

Figure 5 Growth of Trade: Total Trade/GDP (%)

Billions of 1992 dollars

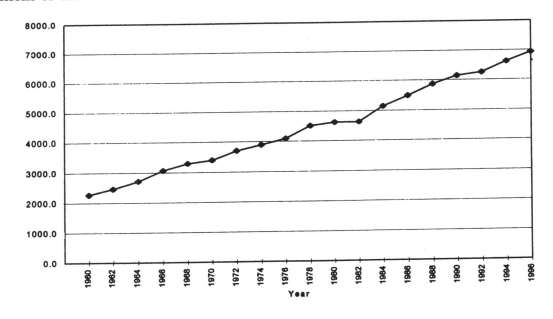

Source: *Economic Report of President*, Table B-2, February 1998.

ACTIVITY 1
PART B

A systematic approach makes the job of deciphering graphs much easier. This activity will help you obtain relevant and important information from Figures 3 and 4 in Activity 1, Part A.

1. Begin with the titles: what information do you expect to find in the graphs?

    Figure 3:_____

    Figure 4:_____

2. The labels on the axes tell what is being measured. What is being measured in each graph?

    Figure 3:_____

    Figure 4:_____

3. What do the graphs tell us has happened to total trade since 1960? To domestic output?

    Total trade since 1960 has:_____

    Domestic output since 1960 has: _____

4. Be careful not to try to read too much into a graph. For example, what can you infer from the graphs about the importance of trade compared to the level of national output?

From *Focus: International Economics*, © National Council on Economic Education, New York, NY.

ANSWERS TO ACTIVITY 1, PART B

This activity will help you obtain relevant and important information from Figures 3 and 4 in Activity 1, Part A. Because of the amount of information they contain, graphs can sometimes be overwhelming. However, a systematic approach makes the job of deciphering graphs much easier.

1. Begin with the titles: What information do you expect to find in the graphs? *Figure 3: The total amount of trade in the United States for the years 1960 until 1996. Figure 4: The total value of Gross Domestic Product for the years 1960 until 1996.*

2. The labels on the axes tell what is being measured. What is being measured in each graph? Figure 3: *The vertical axis is measuring the dollar volume of total trade expressed in constant [1992] dollars. That is, it is real trade showing how much trade there would have been had prices stayed at the level they were at in 1992. The horizontal axis is measuring time in yearly increments from 1960 to the present.* Figure 4: *The vertical axis is measuring the dollar volume of Gross Domestic Product expressed in constant [1992] dollars. That is, it is real Gross Domestic Product showing what the Gross Domestic Product would have been had prices stayed at the level they were at in 1992. The horizontal axis is measuring time in yearly increments from 1960 to the present.*

3. What do the graphs tell us has happened to total trade since 1960? To domestic output? *Total trade since 1960 has increased in real terms. Thus while prices have pushed up the dollar value of total trade, it has increased by more than just the increase in prices. Domestic output since 1960 has also increased in real terms. In fact domestic output has roughly tripled.*

4. One must be careful not to try to read too much into a graph. What can you infer from the graphs about the importance of trade to national output? *Unless you are very good at cross comparisons of graphs, there is not a lot you can tell about the relationship between trade and domestic output, because the absolute amounts of both are increasing rapidly during this time. That is why it is important to construct the table that is asked for in Activity 1, Part C.*

ACTIVITY 1
PART C

Table 1			
Year	Total Trade	GDP	Percentage
1960	194.9	2262.8	8.6
1962	212.5	2454.8	
1964	242.5	2708.9	
1966	287.6	3069.2	
1968	337.8	3293.9	
1970	381.2	3397.6	
1972	433.0	3702.3	
1974	495.1	3891.2	
1976	523.1	4082.9	
1978	611.7	4503.0	
1980	652.7	4615.0	
1982	636.9	4620.3	
1984	784.1	5140.1	
1986	888.3	5487.7	
1988	1046.0	5865.2	
1990	1190.7	6136.3	
1992	1308.4	6244.4	
1994	1529.4	6610.7	
1996	1828.5	6928.4	

All dollar figures in billions of 1992 dollars.

Source: *Economic Report of President*, Table B-2, February 1998

INSTRUCTIONS

1. Complete the percentage calculations in the last column of Table 1 and write a good title for the table in the space provided.

2. Plot the percentage data you have calculated to make a graph on the blank Figure 5 found in Activity 1, Part A.

3. In your own words, write a brief summary of the main points of information presented in Figure 5.

ANSWERS TO ACTIVITY 1, PART C

Figure 5 Growth of Trade: Total Trade/GDP%

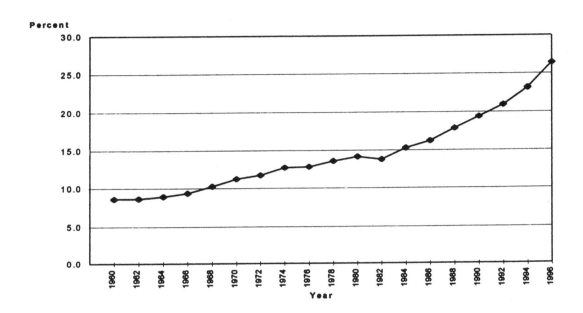

Source: *Economic Report of President*, Table B-2, February 1998.

ANSWERS TO ACTIVITY 1, PART C (continued)

Table 1

Year	Total Trade	GDP	Percentage
1960	194.9	2262.9	8.6
1962	212.5	2454.8	8.7
1964	242.5	2708.9	9.0
1966	287.6	3069.2	9.4
1968	337.8	3293.9	10.3
1970	381.2	3397.6	11.2
1972	433.0	3702.3	11.7
1974	495.1	3891.2	12.7
1976	523.1	4082.9	12.8
1978	611.7	4503.0	13.6
1980	652.7	4615.0	14.1
1982	636.9	4620.3	13.8
1984	784.1	5140.1	15.3
1986	888.3	5487.7	16.2
1988	1046.0	5865.2	17.8
1990	1190.7	6136.3	19.4
1992	1308.4	6244.4	21.0
1994	1529.4	6610.7	23.1
1996	1828.5	6928.4	26.4

All dollar figures in billions of 1992 U.S. dollars

Source: *Economic Report of President*, Table B-2, February 1998.

THE UNITED STATES AND WORLD TRADE

INTRODUCTION

This lesson introduces students to information about the types of goods involved in U.S. trade (exports and imports). It also identifies the major U.S. trading partners and explains key U.S. trade statistics. The lesson again emphasizes how important the concept of opportunity cost is as a factor influencing world trade. Finally, students apply economic reasoning to explain how the observed patterns of trade reflect human preferences, resources, the distances traded goods must travel, and costs imposed by political and cultural constraints. Data presented in this lesson can be updated by reference to the *Survey of Current Business*, published by the U.S. Department of Commerce and found in many libraries.

CONCEPTS

Exports
Imports
Opportunity cost
Cultural and political constraints

CONTENT STANDARDS

When individuals, regions, and nations specialize in what they can produce at the lowest cost and then trade with others, both production and consumption increase.

Comparative advantages change over time because of changes in factor endowments, resource prices, and events that occur in other nations.

Individuals and nations have a comparative advantage in the production of goods or services if they can produce a product at a lower opportunity cost than other individuals or nations.

OBJECTIVES

◆ Use trade statistics to identify the types of goods and services traded by the U.S. and its major trading partners.

◆ Describe how observed patterns can be explained as the result of economic decisions based on costs and incentives.

LESSON DESCRIPTION

Like Lesson Five, this lesson stresses how to read tables, graphs, and statistics that relate to U.S. trade. Students examine graphs on U.S. exports and imports, and the composition of those exports and imports; they use this information to begin to understand the economic factors that influence changes in exports and imports.

TIME REQUIRED

One class period.

MATERIALS

★ One copy of Activities 1 and 2 for each student
★ A transparency of Visual 1

PROCEDURES

1. Distribute copies of Activity 1. As students read over the handout, ask them to form mental pictures of the major types of goods and services represented in the table. Help them to notice the differences in type and quantity of the goods exported and those imported.

2. Have the students determine the percentage of total U.S. exports represented by each of the main headings. As they do so, use their answers to construct a pie chart on the chalkboard. Note: The pie charts are reproduced on Visual 1, should you wish simply to project it as an overhead. (Answer: *Services* = $^{253}/_{870.7}$ X 100 = 29.09%; *Food, feed and beverages = 6.37%; Industrial supplies and materials = 16.19%; Capital goods, except auto = 29.07%; Automotive vehicles, engines and parts = 7.47%; Consumer goods, except auto = 8.05%; Other goods = 2.76%.*)

3. Repeat the exercise, focusing this time on U.S. imports. (*Answer: Services* = $^{156.7}/_{965.6}$ X 100 = 16.23%; *Food, feed and beverages = 3.70%; Industrial supplies and materials, except petroleum = 12.97%; Petroleum and products = 7.53%;*

capital goods, except auto = 23.72%; Automotive vehicles, engines and parts = 13.35%; Consumer goods, except auto = 17.71%; Other goods = 4.81%.)

4. Referring to the pie charts, ask the students to discuss the following questions:

A. Why is the "service component" so large? *(Answer: These consist mainly of tourism and services provided by banks and customers in other countries [such as taking deposits, making loans, and providing financial advice].)*

B. What types of goods does the U.S. mainly export, and why? *(Answer: Food and capital goods, except automotive. The U.S. has a low opportunity cost of growing grains because of our vast land and farm machinery resources. Our technology and industry also make us a low-cost producer of many capital goods, such as commercial passenger jets.)*

C. What types of goods does the U.S. mainly import, and why? *(Answer: Raw materials, vehicles, and consumer goods. These goods can be obtained more cheaply abroad because of foreign resource availability and lower costs of production, including labor.)*

D. Would you expect these percentages to remain constant over time? *(Answer: No. As other nations advance and technologies and prices change, the U.S. may find it cheaper to import and export different commodities. For example, the reduction in the price of crude oil in 1986 cut our total spending on fuel imports dramatically from the levels seen in the 1970s.)*

5. Distribute copies of Activity 2. Have the students fill in the column marked **Total Trade** on Table 2 of the handout. Have them use their figures to identify our top

five trading partners *(Canada, Japan, Mexico, Germany, and China).*

6. Discuss the following questions:

A. Why is our trade greatest with these countries? *(Possible Answers: Physical proximity of Canada and Mexico reduces transportation costs; low-cost consumer goods from Japan and China; free trade agreements [NAFTA and GATT/WTO] have reduced tariffs and other trade barriers; and the relatively high incomes of these countries, other than China, allow them to afford goods produced in the U.S.)*

B. Why is the volume of trade with Eastern Europe and Africa so low, given the size of these areas? *(Possible Answer: The countries in these areas have low incomes, which makes it difficult for them to buy large amounts of any production from any country.)*

7. Ask the students to speculate about what might happen to U.S. exports and imports if the following hypothetical events were to occur.

A. A recession strikes the European Union (EU), greatly reducing these countries' capacities to purchase goods and services. *(Possible Answer: U.S. exports to these countries decline. To the extent that this reduces production and income in our industries, our worldwide imports may also decline.)*

B. The developing countries of Africa begin to experience rapid economic growth, thereby raising the incomes of their citizens. *(Possible Answers: U.S. exports to these economies will likely rise. African consumers will wish to purchase more U.S.-produced goods with their increased wealth.)*

C. China reduces legal restrictions on trading with Western economies. *(U.S. imports and exports will both likely rise.)*

ASSESSMENT

Assign the students to find a graph or chart showing world trade data. in a recent newspaper, and to summarize it accurately and discuss the results

VISUAL 1
EXPORTS AND IMPORTS

Exports

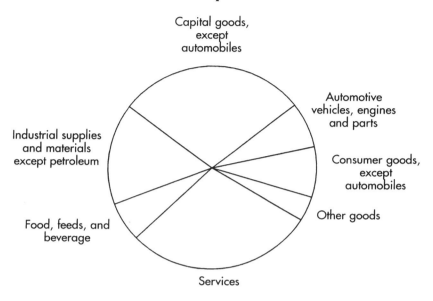

Imports

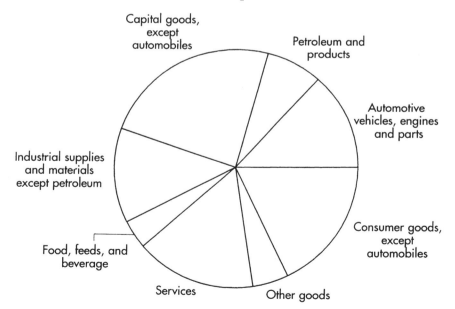

From *Focus: International Economics.* © National Council on Economic Education, New York, NY.

ACTIVITY 1
WHAT DOES THE UNITED STATES TRADE?

In 1996, U.S. exports totaled $870.7 billion. U.S. imports of goods and services totaled $965.6 billion. While many people know that the U.S. exports goods such as corn and airplanes, it is not as widely recognized that there are also exports of services—mostly international banking and finance, and tourism. The major exports and imports of the U.S. in 1996 are summarized in Table 1.

Table 1

U.S. Trade in 1996

Exports		Imports	
Services	253.3	Services	156.7
Food, feeds, and beverage	55.5	Food, feeds, and beverage	35.7
Industrial supplies and materials	141.0	Industrial supplies and materials, except petroleum	125.2
		Petroleum and products	72.7
Capital goods, except automobiles	253.1	Capital goods, except automobiles	229.0
• Civil aircraft and engine parts	30.8	• Civil aircraft and engine parts	12.7
• Computer peripherals and parts	43.7	• Computer peripherals and parts	61.5
• Other	178.6	• Other	154.9
Automotive vehicles, engines, and parts	65.0	Automotive vehicles, engines, and parts	128.90
Consumer goods, except automobiles	70.1	Consumer goods, except automobiles	171.0
Other goods	32.7	Other goods	46.4
	870.7		965.6

All values in billions of U.S. dollars.

Source: *Survey of Current Business*, Table 4.3, January 1998.

ACTIVITY 2
WITH WHOM DOES THE UNITED STATES TRADE?

The U.S. trades goods and services with many other countries. The value of merchandise trade with several of these countries and regions is detailed in Table 2, with the total value of merchandise exports and imports for all countries appearing at the top of each column. The difference between merchandise exports and imports is known as the balance of trade. When the value of imports exceeds the value of exports, a country has a balance of trade deficit. When the value of exports exceeds imports, the country has a balance of trade surplus.

Table 2 1996 U.S. Merchandise Trade: Major Trading Partners

All Countries	Exports $612,069 million	Imports $803,239 million	Total Trade $1,415,308 million
Africa	$ 10,636 million	$ 18,940 million	
Australia	11,705	3,869	
Belgium/Luxembourg	12,685	9,499	
Brazil	12,347	8,773	
Canada	134,609	158,640	
China	11,938	51,511	
Eastern Europe	7,359	7,003	
France	14,454	18,630	
Germany	22,970	38,381	
Hong Kong	13,873	9,854	
Italy	8,621	18,294	
Japan	65,954	115,167	
Korea, Republic of	25,653	22,611	
Mexico	56,735	75,108	
Netherlands	16,501	7,473	
OPEC (Asia)	13,856	21,011	
Singapore	16,253	20,338	
Taiwan	17,540	29,902	
UK	30,246	28,832	
Venezuela	4,665	13,171	

All values are in millions of U.S. dollars.

Source: *Survey of Current Business*, Table 2, January 1998

From *Focus: International Economics*, © National Council on Economic Education, New York, NY.

ANSWERS TO ACTIVITY 2, TABLE 2

Table 2 1996 U.S. Merchandise Trade: Major Trading Partners

All Countries	Exports $612,069 million	Imports $803,239 million	Total Trade (Exports and Imports) $1,415,308 million
Africa	$ 10,636 million	$ 18,940 million	$29,576 million
Australia	11,705	3,869	15,574
Belgium/Luxembourg	12,685	9,499	22,184
Brazil	12,347	8,773	21,120
Canada	134,609	158,640	293,249
China	11,938	51,511	63,449
Eastern Europe	7,359	7,003	14,362
France	14,454	18,630	33,084
Germany	22,970	38,381	61,801
Hong Kong	13,873	9,854	23,727
Italy	8,621	18,294	26,915
Japan	65,954	115,167	181,121
Korea, Republic of	25,653	22,611	48,264
Mexico	56,735	75,108	131,843
Netherlands	16,501	7,473	23,974
OPEC (Asia)	13,856	21,011	34,867
Singapore	16,253	20,338	36,591
Taiwan	17,540	29,902	47,442
UK	30,246	28,832	59,078
Venezuela	4,665	13,171	17,836

All values are in millions of U.S. dollars.

Source: *Survey of Current Business*, Table 2, January 1998

WORLD TRADE

INTRODUCTION

This lesson presents information about international trade in many countries and regions. Students identify the types of goods traded by each country or region, and they speculate about how the observed patterns of trade are the result of comparative advantage, specialization, and economic incentives.

CONCEPTS

Exports
Imports
Comparative advantage
Specialization
Economizing behavior

CONTENT STANDARDS

Voluntary exchange occurs only when all participating parties expect to gain. This is true for trade among individuals or organizations within a nation, and among individuals or organizations in different nations.

Free trade increases worldwide material standards of living.

Imports are foreign goods and services purchased from sellers in other nations.

Exports are domestic goods and services sold to buyers in other nations.

OBJECTIVES

◆ Interpret trade statistics to describe world trade patterns.
◆ Describe how resource distribution, technology, geographic proximity, and cultural/political similarities influence trade patterns.

LESSON DESCRIPTION

In this lesson students observe the patterns and direction of trade. These observations allow them to understand some of the forces that give rise to international trade.

TIME REQUIRED

One class period.

MATERIALS

★ One copy of Activity 1, Parts A and B, for each student
★ One copy of Activity 2, Parts A and B, for each student

PROCEDURES

1. Distribute Activity 1, Parts A and B.

2. To be sure students understand how to read Table 1, ask the following questions:

  A. What was the total amount of Japanese exports to the world in 1996? *($411,242 million)*

  B. What was the total amount imported by all OPEC countries from the rest of the world? *($153,535 million)*

  C. How much did Canada export to the European Union (EU)? *($10,783 million)*

  D. How much did the U.S. import from Japan? *($113,174 million)*

3. Have the students respond to the questions in Activity 1, Part B.

4. Still referring to Activity 1, discuss additional questions:

  A. Why do the bulk of Canadian exports go to the U.S.? *(Suggested Answer: The close proximity of the two countries makes transportation costs low and encourages trade between the two countries. U.S. consumers also earn high incomes, allowing them to buy many imported goods.)*

  B. Why do over half of German and French imports and exports come from countries in the European Union (EU)? *(Suggested Answer: Germany and France are members of the European Union, and trade barriers, which raise trading costs, are much lower between countries within the EU. In addition, geographic proximity is important.)*

5. Distribute Activity 2, Parts A and B.

6. Have the students respond to the questions in Activity 2, Part B.

7. Still referring to Activity 2, discuss additional questions:

A. Why do countries like Japan and the OPEC nations import food? *(Suggested Answer: Their land resources are not well suited for agriculture, so it is cheaper for them to import food.)*

B. What is the major export of the OPEC nations? Why is this? *(Suggested Answer: Oil. The OPEC nations have an abundance of this resource available at very low production costs, compared to oil*

reserves in other parts of the world [such as Alaska and the North Sea].)*

C. Japan and the U.S. primarily export manufactured goods. Why is this? *(Suggested Answer: These countries have an abundance of capital resources, high technology, and skilled labor, which gives them an advantage in the manufacturing of many kinds of goods.)*

D. From the pie charts and our discussion so far, can any generalizations be made about which products a country or region will trade? *(Suggested Answer: Countries export what they can produce cheaply and import what they can produce only at higher opportunity costs.)*

ASSESSMENT

Assess students' answers to the questions on the two handouts and the class discussion of other questions.

ACTIVITY 1, PART A

Table 1 World Trade, 1996 (in millions of dollars)

Importer / Exporter	World	OPEC	European Union	United States	Mexico	Canada	Australia/ New Zealand	Japan	France	Germany
World	5,265,800	153,535	1,919,600	718,042	73,774	171,441	70,458	316,588	269,068	438,919
OPEC	237,300	6,907	50,800	39,342	570	2,393	3,176	44,374	8,254	7,540
European Union	2,041,600	53,384	1,249,100	144,942	6,417	13,494	16,959	44,978	195,010	271,251
United States	622,945	22,380	127,520	-	56,761	132,584	13,649	67,536	14,431	23,474
Mexico	95,991	505	4,543	80,663	-	1,181	61,	1,363	426	641
Canada	200,146	2,290	10,783	164,761	855	-	849	7,471	1,214	2,304
Australia/ New Zealand	75,310	4,700	8,669	5,171	199	1,221	-	14,226	670	1,176
Japan	411,242	17,782	63,136	113,174	3,658	5,124	9,086	-	5,386	18,230
France	289,555	8,794	181,134	17,316	858	1,919	1,591	5,357	-	49,139
Germany	513,472	11,298	289,636	39,927	2,561	2,800	3,999	14,089	55,855	-

Source: *Directions of Trade Statistics Yearbook*, 1997.

ACTIVITY 1, PART B

Refer to Table 1 to answer the following questions:

1. Reading down the first column and across the first row, notice that the total exports of each region are quite close to the same region's total imports. Why is this the case?

2. Why do Mexico and Canada buy the bulk of their imports from the U.S.?

3. Well over half of the European Union's exports and imports are bought from and sold to other countries in the European Union. Why is that so?

ANSWERS TO ACTIVITY 1, PART B

1. A country must export to be able to acquire the funds it needs to import. This is similar to a person working (i.e., selling labor) to acquire money to buy other things.

2. Geographic proximity between the U.S. and these countries makes transportation costs lower, thereby reducing the cost of trade between the U.S. and these countries. In addition, the U.S. is a large producer of many of the products that people in Canada and Mexico want to import.

3. The European Union (EU) trades mainly with itself because the countries within the EU have been politically and economically integrated to eliminate trade barriers. This complete integration began only in 1992, although trade between European countries has always been high, owing to geographic proximity.

ACTIVITY 2, Part A
WHAT GOODS DO COUNTRIES TRADE?

In Lesson Six, U.S. exports and imports of goods and services are broken down into several major categories. Here, the goods exported and imported by four major regions or countries are broken down into several categories and displayed in pie charts. Use this information to answer the questions in Part B of the activity.

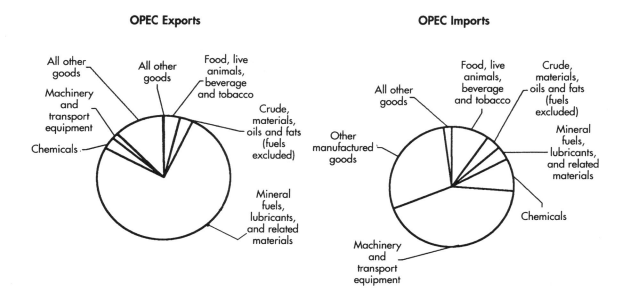

OPEC Exports

All other goods

All other goods

Machinery and transport equipment

Chemicals

Food, live animals, beverage and tobacco

Crude, materials, oils and fats (fuels excluded)

Mineral fuels, lubricants, and related materials

OPEC Imports

Food, live animals, beverage and tobacco

Crude, materials, oils and fats (fuels excluded)

All other goods

Other manufactured goods

Mineral fuels, lubricants, and related materials

Chemicals

Machinery and transport equipment

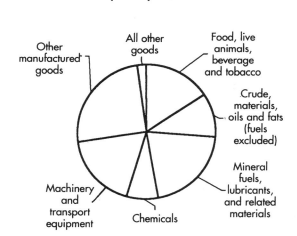

Japan Exports

Machinery and transport equipment

Other manufactured

All other goods

Food, live animals, beverage and tobacco

Crude, materials, oils and fats (fuels excluded)

Mineral fuels, lubricants, and related materials

Chemicals

Japan Imports

Other manufactured goods

All other goods

Food, live animals, beverage and tobacco

Crude, materials, oils and fats (fuels excluded)

Mineral fuels, lubricants, and related materials

Machinery and transport equipment

Chemicals

ACTIVITY 2, Part A (continued)

U.S. Exports

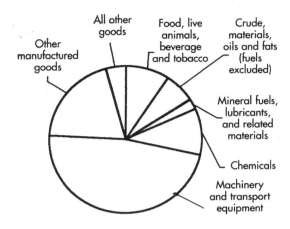

All other goods

Other manufactured goods

Food, live animals, beverage and tobacco

Crude, materials, oils and fats (fuels excluded)

Mineral fuels, lubricants, and related materials

Chemicals

Machinery and transport equipment

U.S. Imports

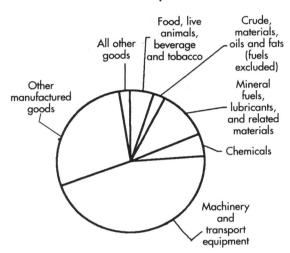

All other goods

Other manufactured goods

Food, live animals, beverage and tobacco

Crude, materials, oils and fats (fuels excluded)

Mineral fuels, lubricants, and related materials

Chemicals

Machinery and transport equipment

Australian/New Zealand Exports

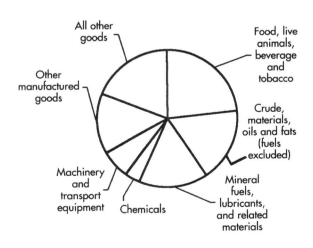

All other goods

Other manufactured goods

Machinery and transport equipment

Chemicals

Food, live animals, beverage and tobacco

Crude, materials, oils and fats (fuels excluded)

Mineral fuels, lubricants, and related materials

Australian/New Zealand Imports

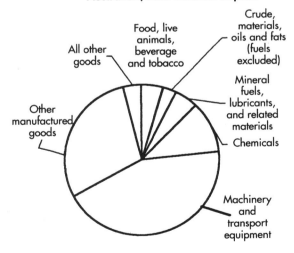

All other goods

Other manufactured goods

Food, live animals, beverage and tobacco

Crude, materials, oils and fats (fuels excluded)

Mineral fuels, lubricants, and related materials

Chemicals

Machinery and transport equipment

ACTIVITY 2, Part B

Refer to Table 1 and the pie charts in Activity 2, Part A, to answer the following questions:

1. Australia/New Zealand are rich in the sort of land needed to produce food and raise cattle, thus making them major exporters of food and live animals. What other example can be found in the pie charts of a country or region having an advantage in the export of an abundant resource?

2. Countries or regions import products that would be expensive for them to produce themselves. For example, OPEC nations import food because of the high expense of producing it domestically. What other examples of this behavior are most obvious in the pie charts?

From *Focus: International Economics*, © National Council on Economic Education, New York, NY.

ANSWERS TO ACTIVITY 2, Part B

1. Oil in the OPEC nations and agricultural products in the U.S. are two examples.

2. Japan (food) and Australia/New Zealand (machinery and transport equipment) are two examples.

TRADE BARRIERS

INTRODUCTION

Most countries make some use of trade barriers, thus reducing trade between people and businesses in the respective countries and people and businesses in other countries. While these barriers reduce the economic well-being of the countries employing them, there are strong incentives for special interest groups to support the adoption of trade barriers. The cost of the trade barriers is spread widely over large numbers of people, making the cost to each individual very small. The benefits are concentrated and received by a very small group of people. Therefore, special interest groups have strong incentives to support trade barriers while most people have little incentive to oppose them. This lesson describes different types of trade barriers and illustrates the gains that can accrue to a small group if the group is successful in imposing a trade barrier.

CONCEPTS

Tariff
Quota
Subsidies
Trade barriers

CONTENT STANDARDS

Costs of government policies sometimes exceed benefits. This may occur because of incentives facing voters, government officials, and government employees, because of actions by special interest groups that can impose costs on the general public, or because social goals other than economic efficiency are being pursued.

Incentives exist for political leaders to implement policies that disperse costs widely over large groups of people and benefit relatively small, politically powerful groups of people.

Although barriers to international trade usually impose more costs than benefits, they are often advocated by people and groups who expect to gain substantially from them. Because the costs of these barriers are typically spread over a large number of people who each pay only a little and may not recognize the cost. policies supporting trade barriers are often adopted through the political process.

When individuals, regions, and nations specialize in what they can produce at the lowest cost and then trade with others, both production and consumption increase.

Transaction costs are costs (other than price) that are associated with the purchase of a good or service. When transaction costs decrease, trade increases.

OBJECTIVES

◆ Distinguish between different types of trade barriers.
◆ Identify who bears the costs and who reaps the benefits of polices that restrict international trade.
◆ Identify incentives that lead political leaders to impose trade barriers.

LESSON DESCRIPTION

Students read definitions of trade barriers, complete a short quiz on trade barriers, work through a short math problem illustrating how trade barriers can serve special interests, and discuss the specific barrier of safety standards for trucks from Mexico.

TIME REQUIRED

Two class periods.

MATERIALS

★ One transparency each of Visuals 1 and 2
★ One copy of Activities 1 and 2 for each student

PROCEDURE

1. Tell students they are going to investigate several policies used to restrict international trade. The effects of some techniques are more obvious than others.

2. Show students Visual 1, **The Mexican Truck Controversy.**

3. Ask students the following questions:

A. Should unsafe trucks from Mexico be allowed into the United States? *(Most students will be opposed to this use of our highways.)*

B. Can a concern for truck safety be used to discourage international trade? *(They may not know the answer to this question. Tell them it will be posed again at the end of the lesson.)*

C. Might you change your mind if you discovered that the truck described was registered to a Texas resident? *(Many students will change their mind and realize they should not be so quick to assume that unsafe trucks are owned only by Mexicans.)*

D. Would you change your mind if you knew that all Mexican trucks had to meet U.S. safety standards in order to cross the border? *(Many students will change their mind once they learn that all drivers and vehicles must abide by U.S. safety standards.)*

E. Do you think that people from the Teamsters Union would change their minds if they knew about the safety standards? *(Students may realize that the Teamsters Union is worried about competition from low-paid Mexican drivers taking jobs away from truckers who are members of the Teamsters Union.)*

4. Ask the students, "What are trade barriers and how do they work to prevent or reduce trade between countries?" To answer this question, students should refer to Activity 1, **Different Kinds of Restrictive Trade Policies**

5. After reading Activity 1, have the students answer the questions on Visual 2—**What Kind of Trade Restriction Is This?** *(Answers, in order, are: tariff, quota, embargo, standards, subsidies.)*

6. Distribute Activity 2, **The Bad Tomato Case.** Ask: Who benefits from trade restrictions? To answer the general question, students should work through the activity in small groups, answering the particular questions (Activity 2, questions 1-13) at the end.

ASSESSMENT

Ask students to review the key ideas of this lesson:

1. Tariffs, quotas, embargoes, standards and subsidies are the main types of trade restrictions.

2. People who benefit from trade restrictions usually are businesses and workers producing products which are protected from foreign competition.

3. People who bear the costs of trade restriction include consumers, import industries, and foreign producers and workers.

VISUAL 1
THE MEXICAN TRUCK CONTROVERSY

News Item:

In 1994, as part of North American Free Trade Act (NAFTA), the U.S. agreed to allow Mexican trucks to enter and travel in this country freely. Mexico also agreed to allow U.S. trucks to enter Mexico and travel in that country without restriction.

December 18, 1995

Action: The Clinton Administration continued the ban preventing Mexican trucks from traveling 20 miles beyond the border into the United States.

Reason: The Clinton administration agreed with concerns raised by the Teamsters Union and other groups who claimed that too many unsafe Mexican vehicles would be traveling on U.S. highways.

"We must first and foremost assure the safety and security of our citizens," said Mickey Kantor, United States Trade Representative.

"The first time there is an accident with one of these Mexican trucks, overloaded and with an unqualified driver, there literally will be hell to pay with the American people," said politician Pat Buchanan.

The following story was reported on the front page of the February 5, 1996 issue of the *Wall Street Journal*:

The green 1969 Chevy truck rattling into this border town looks as if it could be a potent video weapon for an anti-trade group hoping to keep Mexican trucks off U.S. roads. The rusty rig is loaded to the hilt with junk: old car parts, battered steel sheets, metal bars, noxious-looking jars of unknown stuff. The wheels are missing half their lug nuts. The front end lists. The engine clangs suspiciously.

VISUAL 2
WHAT KIND OF TRADE RESTRICTION IS THIS?

Directions: Read the following statements and decide what type of trade barrier is involved. In the blank before the statement, place the appropriate letter to indicate the kind of trade barrier you believe is being described.

T = Tariff, Q = Quota, E = Embargo, St = Standards, Su = Subsidies

_____ 1. China's Most Favored Nation Trading Status will be taken away if Congress and the President agree that the Chinese Government is guilty of human rights abuses. All Chinese imports will experience a sharp increase in taxes if China is no longer considered a Most Favored Nation.

_____ 2. Japanese auto firms agree to limits set in Washington, D.C., on the number of Japanese automobiles that may be sold in the United States.

_____ 3. U.S. State Department officials confirm that the current Administration has decided to continue the prohibition of all U.S. trade with Cuba.

_____ 4. Congress passes a law requiring that all foreign-grown vegetables sold in the United States must be organically grown (no use of chemical fertilizers and herbicides).

_____ 5. U.S. Farmers are allowed to obtain irrigation water from federal dam projects at very low prices to grow rice in the California desert, if they promise to sell 90% of the rice to buyers in Asia.

ACTIVITY 1
DIFFERENT KINDS OF RESTRICTIVE TRADE POLICIES

1. **Tariffs:** A tariff is a tax that must be paid when imports come into a country. For example, if the tariff on imported orange juice is 40%, an orange juice producer from Argentina who wanted to sell $1 million of orange juice in the United States would have to pay $400,000 in taxes to the U.S. Government for the right to sell that orange juice.

2. **Quotas:** A quota limits the amount of a product that can be legally imported into a country. In 1981, the Japanese government and the Japanese automobile industry accepted a "voluntary" quota for Japanese cars to be sold in the United States. This quota reduced the number of Japanese cars sold in the U.S. from 1.82 million in 1980 to 1.68 million in its first year, an 8% reduction.

3. **Embargoes:** An embargo is the complete elimination of trade with people and businesses in a particular country. It is an extreme case of quota, with the quota set at zero. For example, the United States has had an embargo on trade with Cuba for many years.

4. **Subsidies:** This policy reduces costs for producers, often to promote exports to other countries. For example, the U.S. government makes low-cost water available to farmers in eastern Washington state to grow wheat on desert lands. Over 90% of the wheat grown there is exported to other countries.

5. **Standards (Safety and Environmental):** This policy prohibits or restricts the sale of any product that does not meet specific standards set by a government. If these standards are different from those expected of U.S. producers, they serve as trade barriers. This was a heated issue in the debate over NAFTA.

ACTIVITY 2
THE IMPACT OF TRADE BARRIERS ON BUSINESS AND CONSUMERS

Directions: Read the information below and answer the questions that follow.

Imagine you are an investigator hired by the United Nations to monitor trade relations between nations. You are asked to investigate the "Bad Tomato Law" that is upsetting relations between two neighboring countries, Mlorida and Fexico. Mlorida's Parliament just passed a new environmental law outlawing the sale of Fexico's tomatoes in Mlorida. The bill's supporters claimed that Fexico's tomatoes were not grown organically, that too many chemical fertilizers and herbicides were used in their production, and that tomato pickers were exposed to dangerous levels of the herbicides and pesticides while working in the fields. Opponents of the bill, who were small in number, claimed that Fexico's tomatoes and working conditions were no different than Mlorida's. They claimed the environmental issue was just an excuse so Mlorida's tomato farmers would not have to compete with Fexico's tomato farmers. While doing your research, you discover the following facts about the Mlorida tomato industry as it operated before the new law was passed:

1. There are 100 tomato producers in Mlorida.

2. They produce 500,000 cases of tomatoes each year (one case = 25 lbs.)

3. At this time, the Mlorida tomato producers cannot increase their production.

4. Fexico tomato producers sold 500,000 cases of tomatoes each year in Mlorida.

5. There are 10 million tomato consumers in Mlorida.

6. Mlorida consumers bought 1 million cases of tomatoes per year at $25 per case.

You also discover these facts about consequences that followed after the new law was passed:

1. Fexico tomatoes were no longer sold in Mlorida.

2. Tomato prices rose from $25 to $40 per case. Local economists explained that supply declined while demand for tomatoes remained stable, so market prices rose to a new equilibrium level.

3. Mlorida tomato producers continued to produce and sell 500,000 cases of tomatoes per year, but they now charged $40 per case.

You think you may have a story to write (one that has been overlooked by other investigators). But you need to think it through. **Answer the following questions to decide how much the "Bad Tomato Law" has hurt Mlorida consumers.**

1. How many cases of tomatoes were sold per year in Mlorida before the "Bad Tomato Law" was passed?

From *Focus: International Economics*, © National Council on Economic Education. New York, NY.

ACTIVITY 2 (continued)

2 How many cases of tomatoes were sold per year in Mlorida after the "Bad Tomato Law" was passed?

3. What happened to the price of tomatoes after the law was passed?

4. How much total revenue did the Mlorida tomato producers receive before the "Bad Tomato Law" was passed?

5. How much total revenue did the Mlorida tomato producers receive after the "Bad Tomato Law" was passed?

6. How much additional revenue did the Mlorida tomato producers receive as a result of the "Bad Tomato Law"?

7. What is the average amount of extra income that each Mlorida tomato producer receives as a result of the "Bad Tomato Law?"

8. How much extra money must Mlorida consumers pay for Mlorida-grown tomatoes as a result of the "Bad Tomato Law?"

9. For their purchases of Mlorida-grown tomatoes, what is the average additional cost to each Mlorida tomato consumer per year as a result of the "Bad Tomato Law?"

10. If you were a Mlorida tomato producer, would you be willing to pay $5,000 a year to help pay a government lobbyist to work with political leaders to keep Fexico tomatoes out of Mlorida?

11. If you were a Mlorida consumer, would you be willing to pay $5,000 a year to help pay a government lobbyist to work with political leaders to repeal the "Bad Tomato Law?"

12. Given this information, do you think this law will be repealed soon in Mlorida?

13. Reconsider the Mexico truck safety issue. Is it an issue about safety or about trade barriers?

ACTIVITY 2
QUESTIONS & ANSWERS

1. How many cases of tomatoes were sold per year in Mlorida before the "Bad Tomato Law" was passed? *(One million cases)*

2. How many cases of tomatoes were sold per year in Mlorida after the "Bad Tomato Law" was passed? *(500,000 cases)*

3. What happened to the price of tomatoes after the law was passed? *(The price increased from $25 to $40.)*

4. How much total revenue did the Mlorida tomato producers receive before the "Bad Tomato Law" was passed? *(500,000 cases times $25 = $12,500,000)*

5. How much total revenue did the Mlorida tomato producers receive after the "Bad Tomato Law" was passed? *(500,000 cases times $40 = $20,000,000)*

6. How much additional revenue did the Mlorida tomato producers receive as a result of the "Bad Tomato Law"? *($20 million minus $12.5 million = $7.5 Million)*

7. What is the average amount of extra income that each Mlorida tomato producer receives as a result of the "Bad Tomato Law"? *($7.5 Million divided by 100 Producers = $75,000)*

8. How much extra money must Mlorida consumers pay for Mlordia-grown tomatoes as a result of the "Bad Tomato Law"? *($7.5 million, the same as the amount producers receive as extra income.)*

9. For their purchases of Mlordia-grown tomatoes, what is the average additional cost to each Mlorida tomato consumer per year as a result of the "Bad Tomato Law"? *($7.5 million divided by 10 million consumers = 75 cents each.)*

10. If you were a Mlorida tomato producer, would you be willing to spend $5,000 a year to help pay a government lobbyist to work with political leaders to keep Fexico tomatoes out of Mlorida? *(Yes. The cost is $5,000 and the potential gain is $75,000.)*

11. If you were a Mlorida consumer, would you be willing to pay $5,000 a year to help pay a government lobbyist to work with political leaders to repeal the "Bad Tomato Law"? *(No. The cost is $5,000 and the potential gain is only 75 cents)*

12. Given this information, do you think this law will be repealed soon in Mlorida? *(Probably not. The incentives are very strong for businesses to work hard to maintain this tomato ban. On the other hand, although consumers pay more for the tomatoes, the additional cost per consumer is so low that individual consumers have little incentive to be interested in the issue or to fight this political cause.)*

13. Reconsider the Mexico truck safety issue. Is it an issue about safety or about trade barriers? *(It is about both issues, but the more important issue is trade barriers. If the Teamsters are successful in reducing Mexican truck travel in the United States, they can reduce competition in the trucking industry and gain extra income for members of their union.)*

APPENDIX
TRADE BARRIERS: A SUPPLY & DEMAND ANALYSIS

Note to Teacher: This exercise assumes students have already learned the basic principles of supply and demand analysis.

PROCEDURE

1. Draw a graph on the chalkboard with lines representing supply and demand relationships. Tell the students that the following exercise will use graphs like this one to analyze the consequences of trade barriers.

2. Review the basic characteristics and assumptions of these graphs with the students:

   A. Price is measured along the vertical axis.

   B. Output is measured along the horizontal axis.

   C. The upward-sloping supply curve indicates that producers are willing and able to supply more at higher prices.

   D. The downward-sloping demand curve indicates that consumers are willing and able to buy more products at lower prices than at higher prices.

   E. The intersection of the supply and demand lines shows the market equilibrium price and output levels.

3. Ask the students to discuss the determinants of supply which can change the position of the supply curve. Indicate that trade barriers usually alter the supply of a product. Ask students how a trade barrier will shift the supply line, alter the total output, and determine the new market clearing price. Use Visual 1 for the Lesson Eight Appendix to prompt this discussion.

4. Distribute copies of Activity 1 and work through the sample graphical analysis to illustrate how the three graphs work together to provide a complete picture of the total (domestic and foreign) supply of a particular product.

5. Refer to Visual 1 to demonstrate how a tariff changes the market for cotton shirts.

   A. Does the tariff change the supply curve of the goods provided by domestic producer? *(No. Tariffs are paid only by importers, so the domestic supply curve does not change.)*

   B. Does the tariff change the import supply curve? *(Yes. Tariffs represent an increased cost to importers, so the supply curve shifts to the left, indicating that fewer imports are available at any price.)*

   C. Does the tariff change the total supply curve? *(Yes. The total supply curve shifts to the left because the supply of imports has decreased.)*

From *Focus: International Economics*, © National Council on Economic Education. New York, NY.

APPENDIX (continued)

D. Does the tariff change the demand curve? *(No. Increased costs do not change the demand for a good. Increased costs change the supply of goods. Most consumers do not know if there is a tariff on the goods they buy, or when tariffs change.)*

E. Have these changes caused the market clearing price for the total market to change? *(Yes. The new market clearing price [$25] is greater than before.)*

F. Have these changes caused the total output of the market to change? *(Yes. At $25, about 27 million cotton shirts will be sold instead of 30 million.)*

G. How have the changes in the total market altered the price and output in the domestic market graph? *(Domestic producers of cotton shirts can now sell more shirts at higher prices than they could before the tariff was imposed.)*

H. How have the changes in the total market altered the price and output in the import market graph? *(Foreign producers now receive a higher price but sell far fewer cotton shirts than before the tariff was imposed.)*

6. Ask the students who lost and who gained in this example of trade policy. *(Consumers lost, because fewer shirts are available and prices are higher. Importers lost by selling fewer shirts and bearing higher costs. Domestic producers gained by selling more shirts at higher prices.)*

7. Ask students to analyze the questions regarding quotas and subsidies in Activity 1, and to alter the graphs to show the consequences of those trade barriers on price and output. Ask them to follow the process outlined in Visual 1 to find their answers to these problems. Allow students to work in pairs or small teams to complete and check their work.

ASSESSMENT

Review the main points of this Appendix to Lesson Eight:

A. Supply and demand analysis can help people understand the consequences of trade barriers.

B. Quotas and tariffs usually result in increased costs to consumers and lower production levels.

C. Subsidies usually result in greater production and lower prices, but at the cost of increased taxes to taxpayers.

APPENDIX, VISUAL 1
TRADE BARRIERS:
A SUPPLY AND DEMAND GUIDE

To avoid confusion while using supply and demand graphs to clarify the impact of trade barriers, remember two things:

1. Tariffs, quotas, and subsidies change only the supply side of the graph, because trade barriers change the costs of production. If costs are increased, producers reduce supply. (Shifts the supply curve to the left.) If costs are decreased, producers increase supply. (Shifts the supply curve to the right.)

2. A step-by-step, systematic approach reduces the complexity of working with three graphs at the same time. Answering the following questions in order as you complete Activity 1 will make your work less difficult and more rewarding.

Questions

A. Does the tariff change the supply curve of the goods supplied by the domestic producer?

B. Does the tariff change the import supply curve?

C. Does the tariff change the total supply curve?

D. Does the tariff change the demand curve?

E. Have these changes caused the market clearing price for the total market to change?

F. Have these changes caused the total output of the market to change?

G. How have the changes in the total market altered price and output in the domestic market graph?

H. How have the changes in the total market altered price and output in the import market graph?

APPENDIX, ACTIVITY 1
TRADE BARRIERS:
A SUPPLY AND DEMAND ANALYSIS

Exhibit 1

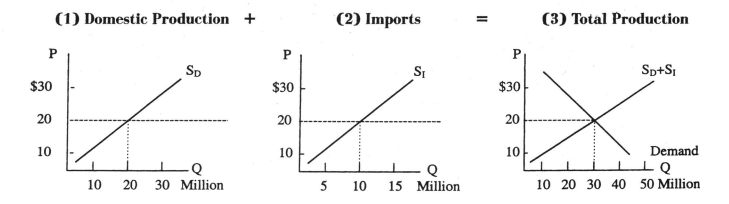

Exhibit 1 contains three graphs which summarize how the total supply of goods like cotton shirts, which are both imported and produced domestically, can be determined. Graph (1) shows the supply of cotton shirts from domestic producers (S_D). Graph (2) shows the supply of cotton shirts from importers (S_I). Graph (3) combines the production of cotton shirts from domestic producers and importers to show a total supply curve for cotton shirts (S_D and S_I). It also includes a demand curve for cotton shirts. The position of the demand curve and the supply curve indicates that the market clearing price is $20 and the amount sold is 30 million shirts. By tracing a straight line back to Graph (1) and Graph (2), we find that at $20 domestic producers will sell 20 million shirts and importers will sell 10 million shirts.

APPENDIX, ACTIVITY 1 (continued)

Exhibit 2

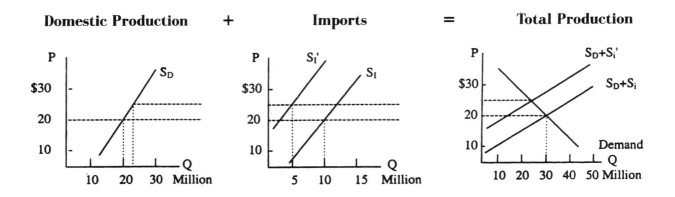

Domestic Production   +   Imports   =   Total Production

Exhibit 2 contains the same three graphs from Exhibit I, changed to illustrate how this situation changes when a tariff is imposed on all imported cotton shirts. This increase in the cost to importers leads to a reduction in the total supply of cotton shirts, which leads to an increase in price ($25). While fewer shirts are sold overall, the rise in price (brought about by a decrease in the supply of imported shirts) leads to an increased production of *domestic* shirts. Thus, both the absolute number of domestic shirts and domestic shirts as a percent of the market increase. Use the questions in Visual 1 to assist you in analyzing this change. Then study the graphs on the following page and try complete them on your own.

APPENDIX, ACTIVITY 1 (continued)

QUOTAS

The three graphs below illustrate a "free trade" situation in the economy. Use the procedures presented in the sample exercise to analyze the impact of the policy changes announced in the following newspaper headline:

QUOTAS IMPOSED! New law passed which limits sales of imported shirts to 5 million!

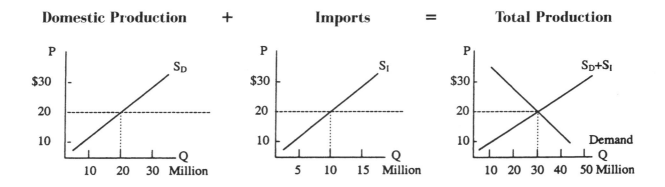

SUBSIDIES

The three graphs below illustrate a "free trade" situation in the economy. Use the procedures provided in the sample exercise to analyze the impact of the policy change announced in the following newspaper headline:

CONGRESS PASSES COTTON SHIRT SUBSIDY! Beginning tomorrow, every domestic manufacturer of cotton shirts will receive $5 for every cotton shirt produced.

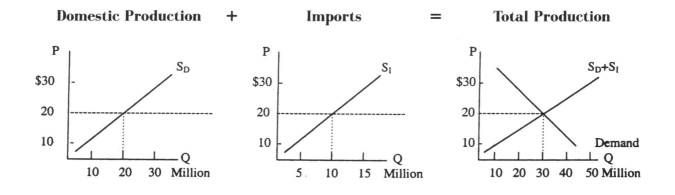

APPENDIX, ACTIVITY 1
ANSWERS

Quotas:

After the quotas, import supply becomes vertical at five units. Beyond that output level and price, any increases in total quantity supplied must come from domestic production. The reduced total supply causes the price to rise, so domestic production rises and imports fall to five units.

Domestic Production

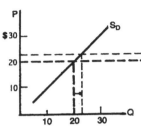

Imports

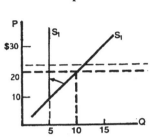

Total

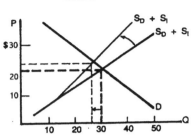

Subsidies:

The subsidy increased domestic supply, and therefore total supply. The resulting lower price causes foreign producers to cut back production.

Domestic Production

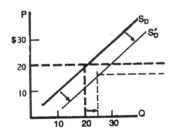

Imports

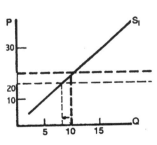

Total

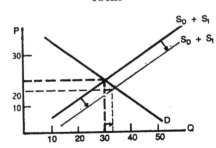

RIPPLES: TRADE BARRIERS AND UNINTENDED CONSEQUENCES

Despite a long-standing and widespread consensus among economists regarding the benefits of free trade in improving living standards domestically and globally, there are strong pressures for political leaders to adopt trade barriers to help some groups of businesses and workers in their countries. The problems (especially higher prices) trade barriers create for consumers of the protected products, including businesses that use those products to produce other goods and services, were described in the previous lesson. In this lesson, the indirect consequences of trade barriers, which are often unexpected because they appear in many markets that seem to have no direct relationship with the protected market, are illustrated.

Business owners and workers in market economies are free to move their resources from the production of one product to another in search of higher profits, wages, or other benefits. When trade barriers create artificially high profit and wage opportunities in protected markets, some firms that have been producing other things, and some workers in these other industries, will leave those markets to pursue new opportunities in the protected markets. That leads to higher price levels for consumers and lower employment levels in the other, unprotected markets. These additional distortions, and others illustrated in this lesson, spread through the economy like the ripples caused when a rock is thrown into a pond. The secondary effects substantially increase the costs of the trade barriers, and offset employment gains in the protected markets.

The overall result is typically no net change in employment, higher prices, less international trade, and a lower standard of living. These negative results occur because trade barriers direct production away from a nation's most efficient and competitive industries to less efficient ones. The inefficient firms will produce more than they otherwise would and perhaps be able to stay in business only because of the special protection they have received through the political process. In most cases such protection can not be continued indefinitely, and the adjustments that occur when the protection eventually fails or is removed are more severe than they would have been before the trade restrictions were adopted.

CONCEPTS
Trade barriers (e.g., tariffs and quotas)
Supply and demand
Special-interest effects

CONTENT STANDARDS
Costs of government policies sometimes exceed benefits. This may occur because of incentives facing voters, government officials, and government employees, because of actions by special interest groups that can impose costs on the general public, or because social goals other than economic efficiency are being pursued.

Although barriers to international trade usually impose more costs than benefits, they are often advocated by people and groups who expect to gain substantially from them. Because the costs of these barriers are typically spread over a large number of people who each pay only a little and may not recognize the cost, policies supporting trade barriers are often adopted through the political process.

OBJECTIVES
◆ Identify both the short-run and long-run effects of trade barriers, and who gains and who loses from such policies.
◆ Recognize that markets are interconnected so that, over time, changes in one market often lead to changes in many other markets.

LESSON DESCRIPTION

First in small groups and then in two large groups, students try to identify which people and organizations would support, or oppose, trade barriers on sugar imports into the United States. When these lists have been completed, the students are given a one-page reading based on a series of *Wall Street Journal* articles dealing with the actual consequences of such trade barriers from 1985-1990. All of the effects are easy to understand after the fact, and some of them were easy enough to predict (these may be reflected in the students' lists). Other effects are much more surprising, affecting markets, people, and organizations seemingly unrelated to the U.S. sugar market. As a general principle, students should recognize that because changes in one market typically lead to a chain reaction in many other markets, it is difficult for policy makers to anticipate all of the effects of trade barriers or other policies that attempt to regulate market activities.

TIME REQUIRED

One class period.

MATERIALS

★ One copy of Activity 1 for each student
★ Several sheets of flip-chart paper or blank overhead transparencies, and two marking pens

PROCEDURE

1. Divide the class into two groups, and divide those two groups into smaller groups of three or four students. Have the groups from the first half of the class make a list of the firms and groups of people who would be likely to support a tariff or quota on sugar that is imported into the United States, and have them list as many benefits of such policies as they can. Have the groups in the second half of the class make a list of the firms and groups of people who would oppose a tariff or quota on sugar imports, and have them list as many costs of such policies as they can. *(Students will often be able to identify the groups most directly affected by the trade barriers. E.g., U.S. sugar cane and sugar beet farmers, and U.S. sugar refining companies, will usually support the tariffs or quotas. They*

will benefit from the decrease in supply of foreign sugar and the increase in demand for U.S. sugar, which will lead to higher prices, profits, and output and employment levels for the U.S. sugar industry. On the other hand, the higher prices for sugar will hurt U.S. sugar consumers and the foreign companies and foreign workers who produced sugar that was sold in the U.S. It is possible that students will also identify some of the groups who are helped or harmed by the secondary effects of the trade barriers [see Activity 1, which will be distributed to students later in the lesson], but it is very unlikely that they will identify all of these effects.)

2. Arrange for the groups that listed the supporters and advantages of the tariffs or quotas to meet together, to prepare one master list to present to the full class. If some groups listed supporters or advantages that other groups did not, have them explain their reasoning to the other groups, and then discuss whether or not to include the new items on the combined list. Have the students prepare a good copy of their final list on a sheet of flip-chart paper or an overhead transparency. Do the same thing with the groups that listed the opponents and disadvantages of the tariffs or quotas.

3. Assign the groups to choose speakers to present and explain the master lists prepared in procedure 2. After these presentations, see if any students from either half of the class can add additional items to either list. Let all of the students discuss whether or not a suggested item should be added to a list, and whether any of the items that were included on either list should be removed. When the class agrees on the final version of the two lists, conduct a straw poll to see how many students would favor a tariff or quota on imported sugar, and how many would oppose the trade barriers.

4. Distribute one copy of Activity 1 to each student. This activity is based on a series of *Wall Street Journal* articles dealing with the effects of U.S. trade barriers on imported sugar that appeared on September 26, 1986 (pp. 1, 20), October 9, 1986 (p. 39), December 16,

1986 (p. 14), and July 26, 1990 (pp. 1, 11). After students have read the activity sheet, have them modify the two lists they prepared in Procedures 2 and 3 to add any benefits/supporters and costs/opponents they failed to list. Then conduct another straw poll to see how many students now support or oppose the trade barriers, and note whether the vote changed. *(In classes where the case for free trade has been made in earlier lessons, it is possible that most or all of the class will vote to oppose the trade barriers before and after reading Activity 1. On the other hand, classes in areas where employment has been adversely affected by increased competition from imports may have many students who continue to favor trade barriers. In these cases,* *discuss how the material in Activity 1 has affected the intensity of students' support for, or opposition to, trade barriers.)*

ASSESSMENT

Have students research the history of trade barriers in the U.S. and/or Australian automobile industries in the 1980s, and compare and contrast the effects of those trade barriers with the trade barriers on sugar that were discussed in this lesson. Be sure to identify the groups that were helped and hurt by these import restrictions.

ACTIVITY 1
TRADE BARRIERS FOR SUGAR ATTRACT MORE FLIES

When the United States federal government limited the amount of sugar that could be imported from other nations, sugar cane and sugar beet farmers in Louisiana, Hawaii, Colorado, and other states were understandably happy. Sugar prices in the U.S. soared to more than twice the world price. That made U.S. companies that refined sugar more profitable, too, so they refined more sugar and hired more workers. That was exactly what the trade barriers were designed to do. But the trade barriers also caused many other things to happen—some of them good, some of them very bad.

First, the higher sugar prices were bad news for U.S. sugar consumers, including many companies that used sugar to produce other goods (such as candy, soft drinks, and breakfast cereals). The higher cost for sugar led to price increases for the products made with sugar, and the higher prices resulted in decreased sales, output, and employment levels in these firms. Many of these companies switched to sugar substitutes, such as sweeteners made from corn. That was good news for U.S. corn farmers in states like Indiana and Illinois, and for companies that refined the corn sweetener from corn. These farmers and firms now joined the sugar farmers and sugar refining companies in supporting the trade barriers on imported sugar.

Other effects were felt far away from the United States, and these effects were almost always bad news. For example, sugar companies and workers in the Caribbean were hurt because most of the sugar they produced had been sold in the United States. Now, with the trade barriers sharply reducing the amount of sugar they could sell in the United States, less sugar was grown and refined, and many workers were laid off. Some of these former sugar growers and workers switched to other products that were still being sold in the United States, including marijuana. Illegal immigration from the Caribbean to the United States also increased as the unemployment rate rose among unskilled workers who had worked on the Caribbean sugar farms.

Back in the United States, the higher prices for sugar led more farmers to grow sugar cane, sugar beets, and corn, but to do that they had to plant less wheat and soybeans. That allowed foreign producers to grow more wheat and soybeans. Some observers pointed out that the trade barriers on sugar put more U.S. farmland into sugar products that could be grown at a lower cost in other countries, and less U.S. farmland into wheat and soybeans, even though these crops could be grown at a lower cost here than in other countries. Many worried that when the sugar trade barriers were removed, the increased foreign competition in wheat and soybean markets would not disappear. The higher prices for sugar, corn, and other agricultural products also increased rents on U.S. farm land.

DISCUSSION QUESTIONS:

1. In the U.S., who was hurt and who was helped by the trade barriers on sugar?

2. In the Caribbean, who was hurt and who was helped by the trade barriers on sugar?

WHAT HAPPENS HERE WHEN IMPORTS ARE BANNED?

INTRODUCTION

Policies that close a domestic market to imported goods divert international trade away from patterns that would exist in a free-trade setting. This can have an impact on where certain goods will be produced and consumed. The result may be a distortion of world production and decreased levels of consumption. With such decreases, standards of living will be lower than they would have been under conditions of free trade. This lesson describes a classroom exercise designed to illustrate the effects of closing a domestic market to imported goods.

The exercise is conducted in two stages. In stage 1, a system of free trade is in effect—any producer can trade with any consumer in either country. In stage 2, an import quota is adopted, making it impossible for consumers in country A to buy goods produced in country B. Students compare the levels of consumption and production in the two countries in the two stages. The comparison allows them to understand efficiency losses from trade barriers and to see which segments of society benefit and which are hurt by restricting imports. This analysis should help students understand the political forces working for and against trade restrictions.

CONCEPTS

Import quotas
Free trade
Production
Consumption

CONTENT STANDARDS

Costs of government policies sometimes exceed benefits. This may occur because of incentives facing voters, government officials, and government employees, because of actions by special interest groups that can impose costs on the general public, or because social goals other than economic efficiency are being pursued.

Citizens, government employees, and elected officials do not always directly bear the costs of their political decisions. This often leads to policies whose costs outweigh their benefits for society.

Although barriers to international trade usually impose more costs than benefits, they are often advocated by people and groups who expect to gain substantially from them. Because the costs of these barriers are typically spread over a large number of people who each pay only a little and may not recognize the cost, policies supporting trade barriers are often adopted through the political process.

When individuals, regions, and nations specialize in what they can produce at the lowest cost and then trade with others, both production and consumption increase.

Transaction costs are costs (other than price) that are associated with the purchase of a good or service. When transaction costs decrease, trade increases.

OBJECTIVES

◆ Identify the effect of closing a domestic market (by restricting imports) on firms in the home country, and on firms in foreign countries that were exporting those products.
◆ Identify the impact of an import restriction on consumption levels in the country imposing the quota and in the world as a whole.

LESSON DESCRIPTION

Students participate in a classroom exercise followed by a classroom discussion in which they act as producers and consumers in a two-country economy. The exercise is designed to isolate the effects of import restrictions on production and consumption patterns.

Students assume roles as either consumers or producers in one of two countries, country A or

LESSON TEN

country B. Producers in either country can choose to produce one of two commodities: chocolate bars or boxes of raisins. Producers in country A are more efficient producers of chocolate bars than producers in country B. Producers in country B are more efficient producers of raisins than producers in country A. Consumers in both countries want to purchase both products. Producers in both countries would like to sell their products at the highest prices they can.

TIME REQUIRED

Approximately two class periods.

MATERIALS

★ One copy of Activity 1 for each student.

★ Candy bars and small boxes of raisins. The quantity of each good should be at least three-quarters of the total number of students in the class. These items are used both as the goods traded in the exercise and as prizes awarded to traders who make the best buying and selling decisions during the exercise.

★ 100 dollars of monopoly money per student, denominated in small bills.

PROCEDURE

1. Before the class period, familiarize yourself with the procedures explained in Activity 1.

2. At the beginning of the class period, divide the students into four groups of equal number. If the total number of students is not divisible by four, put some of the students into teams of two or more, but be sure that the number of teams is divisible by four. Identify the four groups as (i) consumers in country A, (ii) consumers in country B, (iii) producers in country A, and (iv) producers in country B.

3. Distribute Activity 1. Fill in the two blanks appropriately for each student.

4. Read the Activity aloud for the students. Ask them to follow along on their copies as you are reading. Tell them to feel free to ask any questions.

5. The activity takes place in six rounds. Six rounds are used because it usually takes several rounds for the market to stabilize. (You may want to make the first round a practice round, or conduct an extra round, with the first of seven rounds serving as a practice round.) The first three rounds make up phase 1 of the exercise, in which free trade between countries A and B can take place. The last three rounds make up phase 2, in which producers in B are not allowed to sell their export to consumers in country A. At the start of each round, give 100 dollars of monopoly money to each consumer. At the end of each round, take the money back from the students, and use that money to give $100 to each consumer at the start of the next round.

6. **Production.** At the beginning of each round, ask each producer in country A to choose whether he wishes to produce two chocolate bars or one box of raisins during that round. Ask each producer in country B to choose whether he wishes to produce one chocolate bar or two boxes of raisins for the round. Give each producer the appropriate quantity of the good he or she has chosen to produce.

7. **Consumption.** Then give producers and consumers an opportunity to bargain with each other and to conduct trades. Consumers may only buy from producers and producers may only sell to consumers, and no speculation (buying for purposes of resale) is permitted. The length of the time period for bargaining in each round should be roughly 5 minutes for classes of up to 30 students. (More time is probably needed for larger groups.) When a producer and a consumer have agreed to a trade, they must inform the instructor, who records the trade on the blackboard as in the example in Figure 1. The trade counts only if it is posted on the blackboard.

82

Figure 1: Blackboard Display #1

Period	Good	Consumer's Name	Consumer's Country	Producer's Name	Producer's Country	Price
1	Raisins	Mary	A	Joe	B	$21*

**Possible Result*

Leave the information in Figure 1 posted on the board for the entire class period.

8. After trading is concluded for the round, record how many consumers in each country were able to purchase both a chocolate bar and a box of raisins, and post this information on the board as illustrated in Figure 2. Also, record the total production of each good in each country on the blackboard. Record the name of the consumer in each country who was able to purchase a unit of both goods at the lowest cost and record the name of the producer with the greatest cash amount (profit) at the end of the round in each country. These are the four winners for the round.

Figure 2: Blackboard Display #2

Period	Number of Consumers in A Purchasing Both Goods	Number of Consumers in B Purchasing Both Goods	Amount of Production of Choc. Bars in A	Amount of Production of Choc. Bars in B	Amount of Production of Raisins in A	Amount of Production of Raisins in B
1	4*	5*	8*	1*	0*	10*

**Possible Results*

9. Repeat procedures 6-8 two more times, for a total of three rounds in phase 1. Keep all of the information from earlier rounds on the blackboard.

10. At the beginning of the fourth round, announce that consumers in country A are no longer permitted to purchase goods from producers in country B. Write the following sentence on the chalkboard: "From this point on, producers in country B may not sell to consumers in country A."

11. Run three more rounds, with this restriction in place throughout all three rounds. Record information on trading, production levels, and prices exactly as in rounds 1-3.

12. After the sixth round, discuss the issues outlined in the assessment section below.

13. Award the prizes of chocolate bars and boxes of raisins to the winning students. There are four winners per period.

ASSESSMENT

After the exercise is completed, compare the quantity of each good produced in each country before and after the import restriction was imposed. Also compare the total number of agents in each country who were able to buy a unit of both commodities. Discuss the following questions (brief suggested answers are given for each question):

Question 1. Under free trade, which country produced more chocolate bars? Which country produced more raisins? Why? *(Suggested Answer: In theory, country A should produce only chocolate bars and country B should produce only boxes of raisins. If all goes as planned in the exercise, by round three A should be producing more chocolate bars than B, and B should produce more boxes of raisins than A. Country A was most likely an exporter of chocolate bars, and country B was an exporter of raisins. According to the theory of comparative advantage, this pattern is a result of the fact that country A produces chocolate bars more cheaply in terms of raisins forgone than B does. Country A produces two chocolate bars for each box of raisins, whereas B produces one chocolate bar for every two boxes of raisins.)*

Question 2. How did banning imported raisins in country A affect the amount of each good that country A produced? How did it affect the amount of each good produced in B? *(Suggested Answer: Producers in A probably began to produce more raisins and fewer chocolate bars under the import ban than under free trade. Since consumers in A could no longer buy raisins from B, they would be willing to pay higher prices to buy raisins from producers in A, presenting profit opportunities for producers in B. Producers in B most likely produced more chocolate bars and fewer raisins than before. Because they could no longer export raisins, and they would produce more than were wanted in the domestic market if they all produced raisins, it is a good strategy for some producers in A to switch to producing chocolate bars. The* fact that some producers in A switch production from chocolate bars to raisins opens up opportunities for producers in B to sell chocolate bars to consumers in B.)

Question 3. How did banning raisin imports into country A affect total world production of each of the two goods? *(Suggested Answer: World production of each of the goods was probably reduced. Under free trade, we would expect that all producers in A would produce chocolate bars, and all producers in B would produce raisins. This would be enough output to ensure that all consumers could buy one unit of each good. However, with the import restriction in effect, some producers in each country have an incentive to switch to producing the other good, which they cannot produce as efficiently. That reduces world production of both goods.)*

Question 4. How did the import ban affect the number of consumers in country A who were able to buy both goods? How did it affect the number of consumers in country B who could buy both goods? *(Suggested Answer: Under free trade, there is enough production for every consumer to purchase both goods. However, with the import restriction it is impossible for all of the consumers in A to purchase both goods, because they cannot buy imports from B. Consumers in B can still buy both goods, but owing to reduced world production the number of consumers in the world who can consume both goods is lower than it would be under free trade.)*

Question 5. Now imagine that you are a worker in country A who only knows how to make raisins. Would you support lifting the ban on the importation of goods from country B to allow free trade? *(Suggested Answer: If you are a worker making raisins, you are better off if there are more raisins produced in your country. Under free trade, country A doesn't make raisins because the competition from B is too tough, but if the ban on imports from B is in effect, country A makes raisins. Therefore, you would probably support the ban.)*

Question 6. Now suppose that you were a consumer in country A. Would you support lifting the ban on the importation of goods from country B? *(Suggested Answer: Consumers in A are better off under free trade. They are more likely to be able to purchase both goods, especially the boxes of raisins, which are produced more efficiently by country B than country A.)*

Question 7. Suppose there was a proposal to ban automobile imports into the U.S. Which groups in the U.S. would you expect to support this ban, and which ones would oppose it? *(Suggested Answer: Imagine that the boxes of raisins in the exercise represent cars, and that country A represents the U.S. U.S. auto workers and auto firms would support the import ban because it would tend to increase the quantity of cars produced in the U.S. Consumers of autos would oppose the ban because it would be harder to buy cars at affordable prices.)*

ACTIVITY 1
WORLD TRADE SIMULATION

You have been assigned as a resident of one of two countries, country A or country B. You are a resident of country_____. You have also been assigned as either a producer or a consumer. You are a_____. The exercise will take place in several different rounds.

Instructions for Consumers: At the beginning of each round, you will receive an income of 100 dollars (in monopoly money) which you can use to purchase a chocolate bar and a box of raisins from producers.

Your objective is to purchase one chocolate bar and one box of raisins, and to have as much money left over as possible. You are not allowed to buy more than one chocolate bar or more than one box of raisins in any given round.

The consumer in each country who has the most money left at the end of the round, and who has also been able to purchase one chocolate bar and one box of raisins, is allowed to keep his/her choice of chocolate bar or box of raisins after the exercise.

Instructions for Producers: At the beginning of each round you will be asked to choose whether you would like to produce chocolate bars or boxes of raisins in the period. If you are a producer in country A, you can produce either two chocolate bars or one box of raisins. If you are a producer in country B, you can produce either one chocolate bar or two boxes of raisins.

You may sell what you produce to any consumer who wishes to buy it. If you produce two units you do not have to sell them both to the same consumer. You may sell to consumers in either country.

The money you receive from your sales is your profit for the round. The producer in each country who has the most cash at the end of the round gets to keep his or her choice of a chocolate bar or a box of raisins after the exercise.

There will be a total of six rounds. Good luck!

BALANCE OF PAYMENTS

INTRODUCTION

Each month, newspapers report information about the balance of trade accounts for the United States. In recent years, they typically have reported that the balance of trade was in deficit. There are also occasional reports about the balance of payments, the current account, and capital flows. Students who hear or read about these various balances are often confused, or have no idea at all what these different balances mean. It is also difficult for them to see what influence these measures have on the overall economy, and ultimately on them.

In this lesson, the balance of payments for the U.S. economy for each of two years is presented. By analyzing the relevant data, students will understand the various components of the balance of payments. And looking at changes in the accounts over two years will help show how economic events influence the balance of payments.

We present the balance of payments accounts table in a form that shows which transactions lead to a demand for the U.S. dollar, and which ones lead to a supply of dollars on world currency markets. That same approach is used in later lessons that discuss currency markets and exchange rates. The appendix explains this perspective on the components of balance of payments.

CONCEPTS

Balance of payments
Current account
Capital account deficits and surpluses

CONTENT STANDARDS

Voluntary exchange occurs only when all participating parties expect to gain. This is true for trade among individuals or organizations within a nation, and among individuals or organizations in different nations.

Imports are foreign goods and services purchased from sellers in other nations.

Exports are domestic goods and services sold to buyers in other nations.

A nation pays for its imports with its exports.

Markets exist when buyers and sellers interact. This interaction determines market prices and thereby allocates scarce goods and services.

Relative price refers to the price of one good or service compared to the prices of other goods and services. Relative prices are the basic measures of the relative scarcity of products when prices are set by market forces (supply and demand).

OBJECTIVES

◆ Understand the difference between the balance of trade and the balance of payments.
◆ Explain how each component in the balance of payments account influences the demand for dollars and the supply of dollars.
◆ Understand the relationship between the current account and the capital account.

LESSON DESCRIPTION

Students learn the basic components of the balance of payments and what it means to have a balance of trade surplus or deficit, a current account surplus or deficit, a capital account surplus or deficit, a balance of payments surplus or deficit, and how deficits are ultimately paid for. They see that a current account deficit results when imports exceed exports, or when capital inflows exceed capital outflows. Overheads or readings with balance of payments accounts are given to students. Then, in question and discussion sessions, students learn about the various components of these accounts.

TIME REQUIRED

Two class periods.

MATERIALS

★ One transparency each of Visuals 1 and 2
★ One copy of Activity 1 for each student

PROCEDURE

1. Display Visual 1, which is a listing of the U.S. balance of payments accounts for 1996, on the overhead projector.

    A. Ask students if they know what it means to export a good or service. *(Sell it abroad.)*

    B. Do they know what it means to import a good or service? *(Buy it from abroad.)*

    C. From looking at the overhead, can they tell how many goods and services U.S. producers sold abroad and how many goods and services U.S. citizens bought from abroad in 1996? *(U.S. citizens sold [exported] $836 billion and bought [imported] $950 billion.)*

    D. Did we sell more abroad or buy more abroad? What commonly cited figure in the news have they just calculated? *(We bought more abroad than we sold; this is measured by the balance of trade, and when we import more than we export, we say there is a* **balance of trade deficit**.*)*

    E. When the U.S. sells abroad, do U.S. producers want payments in dollars or in foreign currency? *(Dollars)*

    F. When the U.S. buys abroad, do foreigners want payments in their home currency or in dollars? *(They want payment in their home currency. Students who have traveled abroad may have noted that some stores will take payment in dollars. However, unless the shopkeeper is planning to travel to the U.S., he or she is likely to take those dollars to a local bank and exchange them for the home currency. In doing this, the exchange rate the shopkeeper receives at the bank is often better than the rate given to the hapless American. There are some countries where dollars are held due to high inflation of the domestic currency and political instability. But normally, for most countries that the*

U.S. trades with, people and firms in other countries do not want to hold dollars and must be paid in their home currency.)

    G. How do U.S. sellers get payment in dollars when they sell goods and services abroad? *(Either they make their buyers exchange their local currency for dollars, or they make these exchanges after they are paid in another currency. The important thing that you want to get from this discussion is that whenever someone from the U.S. exports goods abroad, the export leads to a demand for dollars when the foreign currency is traded to buy dollars. On the other hand, whenever someone from the U.S. buys goods abroad, that leads to a supply of dollars in the international market, as dollars are traded to purchase foreign currency.)*

    H. Looking at the deficit on the balance of trade for 1996, did that lead to a net demand or a net supply of dollars in the market? *(We can think of all of the items in the balance of trade accounts as leading to a demand for or supply of dollars in international markets. This differs from the traditional approach of looking at a debit and credit approach on the balance of trade, but it makes more sense intuitively to many students. A deficit on any account that is a component of the balance of trade will lead to a net supply of dollars in the market. Likewise, a surplus on any of the accounts will lead to a net demand for dollars in the international market.)*

    I. Compare the 1996 trade balance with the 1994 trade balance shown in Visual 2. Did the U.S. supply more dollars on net in 1994 or 1996? *(1996)*

2. Point out that under the Current Account, line number 2 is Interest and Dividends to U.S. holders of foreign financial assets. Ask students the following questions:

A. If a U.S. citizen holds either a foreign bond or a foreign stock, in what currency are the interest and dividend payments made? *(The payment is made in the domestic currency of the issuing country, but when that check is written to a U.S. citizen, that individual takes the check to a bank somewhere and presents it for payment in dollars. In doing this, that person is **demanding dollars**.)*

B. If a foreigner owns a stock or bond issued by a U.S. company, what currency are his or her interest and dividend checks written in? *(Interest and dividend checks are written in dollars. However, just as the U.S. citizen will turn in the foreign-denominated check for dollars, the foreigner will turn in the dollar-denominated check for his or her home currency. Students may not be aware that a fairly large amount of the national debt of the United States is held by foreigners. When the U.S. government makes interest payments on the U.S. debt to those foreigners who hold the debt, they contribute to the current account deficit.)*

C. Compare the net demand for dollars in the category Interest and Dividends to holders of foreign financial assets for 1996 and 1994. Has there been a large change? *(There is not much change from 1994 to 1996.)*

D. The category Transfers (gifts and government grants) shows a deficit for both 1994 and 1996. What does this mean in terms of the supply and demand for dollars and the actions of the United States? *(A deficit in this account means that the U.S. is supplying more dollars than are being demanded. This means the U.S. gave more money to other countries as gifts than were given to the U.S.)*

E. The trade, interest, and transfer accounts summed together are known as the current account. Was the current account in surplus or deficit in 1994 and 1996? What does that imply about the demand for and supply of dollars in currency markets in those years? *(The current account was in deficit for both years. That means that the US was supplying more dollars in the market than were being demanded in those years.)*

3. Line 4 in Visual 1 is the capital account. It shows the amounts of capital that flowed in and flowed out of the United States in 1996. The capital account also includes the amount we both borrow abroad and lend abroad.

A. If the U.S. borrows money from abroad, does that result in a capital inflow or a capital outflow? Does that increase or decrease the demand for or supply of dollars? *(When the U.S. borrows from abroad there is a capital inflow — i.e., capital flows into the U.S. This results in a demand for dollars as the U.S. firms in which foreigners invest want dollars. Thus, foreigners must convert their home currency to dollars)*

B. If the U.S. lends abroad, is that a capital inflow or outflow? Does that increase or decrease the demand for or supply of dollars? *(There is a capital outflow — U.S. citizens and firms supply dollars in the international market.)*

C. Ask the students to give examples of each to make certain they understand the concept. (If a foreigner buys a U.S. treasury bond, stock on the NYSE, or decides to purchase a building in Manhattan, there is a capital inflow and a demand for dollars. If any of the opposite transactions occur, there is a capital outflow and a supply of dollars.)

D. What was the position of the capital account in 1996, 1994? Does this mean the U.S. borrowed from abroad or lent abroad? Is this good or bad? *(The capital account was in surplus in both years, $121 billion in 1994 and $89 billion in 1996. That means that the U.S.*

borrowed from abroad. The impact of a current account deficit and how that might be interpreted in terms of economic activity is covered in the discussion of the reading used in the assessment section.)

4. After accounting for statistical discrepancies we come to the figure for the balance of payments. The balance of payments (before official transactions) was in deficit for each of the years listed 1994 and 1996.

   A. What was the size of the deficit in each of these years *($128 billion in 1996 and $44 billion in 1994.)*

   B. What explains most of the difference in the size of the deficit in those two years? *(There was a larger capital inflow in 1994 than there was in 1996.)*

   C. What happens to dollars that are in excess supply when the U.S. runs a balance of payments deficit? *(They are either bought by a foreign country's monetary authorities or the U.S. monetary authorities buy them up.)*

   D. How does the Central Bank buy them up? Can it do this indefinitely? *(A central bank buys up its currency in the foreign market with foreign currency reserves it obtains from having run surpluses some time in the past. If a country runs a persistent balance of payments deficit and runs out of foreign reserves, it is forced to go to the International Monetary Fund to borrow funds to support its deficit. You sometimes read in the paper about the IMF telling a country it has to control its fiscal and monetary policies. The IMF can tell a country to do this if the country owes the IMF.)*

ASSESSMENT

Have the students read Activity 1, which is the first page from a monthly report published by the St. Louis Federal Reserve Bank, *International Economic Trends*. (Publications from the various Federal Reserve Banks are free. The St. Louis Fed publishes monthly reports with many helpful charts, graphs, and reports. Single-copy subscriptions are available free of charge by writing to the Public Affairs Office, Federal Reserve Bank of St. Louis, Post Office Box 442, St. Louis, MO 63166-0422, or by calling (314) 444-8808 or (314) 444-8809.) After students have read the article, discuss the following questions.

   A. The U.S. had a current account deficit of $165 billion in 1996 and $167 billion in 1987. If those figures were reversed, would it be correct to say that the current account deficit in 1996 is the largest ever? *(Not in real terms. Remind students of the distinction between real and nominal values. The current account numbers should be scaled in some way, such as looking at them as a percentage of GDP. The article shows those figures, too.)*

   B. When the U.S. had a current account deficit, what was happening on the capital account? *(A deficit on the current account means there is a surplus on the capital account.)*

   C. What does the current account deficit say about the relationship between spending and saving in the United States? *(It means the U.S. spends more than it saves, and has to borrow from abroad. Remember, a surplus on the capital account means there is a net capital inflow, as U.S. citizens borrow from abroad.)*

   D. Does this mean the U.S. lacks competitiveness in global markets? *(Maybe, but not necessarily. The fact that we borrow abroad may also reflect the fact that the U.S. offers good opportunities for investing by foreigners. Some analysts say that the current account deficit means that we buy too many goods abroad. This is essentially a protectionist approach, and other lessons in this volume discuss the costs and benefits of protection. This lesson only discusses the impact of such deficits on the balance of payments.)*

E. Is it good or bad that the U.S. borrows from abroad? *(It depends. The fact that the U.S. borrowed abroad means it spent more than it saved. If spending was for consumption goods, then the U.S. is like the grasshopper from the Aesop's fable and that is bad. If it borrowed abroad in order to invest more, that is no different from a company borrowing for investment purposes. Because a current account deficit is associated with imports exceeding exports, individuals often associate it with consumption spending, a loss of jobs, and a "lack of competitiveness" for the U.S. That need not be the case, however, because a current account deficit may also reflect a strong atmosphere for investing in the U.S., which leads to a capital account surplus.)*

F. What is the recent evidence for the U.S. concerning how it uses funds borrowed from abroad? *(Because real fixed investment spending and spending on consumer durables have been rising at a more rapid rate than real GDP, the evidence suggests that a strong environment for investment largely explains the capital account surplus and the current account deficit.)*

APPENDIX

This Appendix provides another suggestion on how to go through the material on the balance of payments, and additional background information about what each of the accounts measures. Begin by going to the chalkboard and drawing a map of the United States and a map of Europe. About half way between the U.S. and the European continent, draw Iceland, with a spot for the city of Reykjavik where the (possibly fictional) Bank of Reykjavik is located. These drawings do not need to be neat and exact; inexact drawings may lighten the mood. Pretend that there is a Bank of Reykjavik and that all international transactions must run through that Bank. We start with the assumption that foreigners do not want to hold dollars in the long run any more than U.S. citizens want to hold foreign currency. Any time people find themselves with foreign currency, they take it to the Bank of Reykjavik for exchange. Some students who have traveled abroad or whose parents have traveled abroad may have difficulty with this concept, because they may have seen or heard of foreigners accepting U.S. dollars. The important point to make here is that the foreigners will not hold that currency forever, but will eventually trade it for their own currency. That trade must take place at the Bank of Reykjavik.

Each time an individual goes to the Bank of Reykjavik and uses foreign currency to buy U.S. dollars, that represents a demand for dollars. Each time a U.S. citizen goes to the Bank to purchase foreign currency, that represents a supply of dollars. Students should realize that a demand for dollars means someone is supplying foreign currency. Likewise a supply of dollars means someone is demanding a foreign currency.

Looking at items in the balance of payments accounts demonstrates which transactions give rise to a demand for dollars at the Bank of Reykjavik and which give rise to a supply of dollars. After your students understand what creates a demand for and supply of dollars, they

are ready to discuss accounting issues in the balance of payments for 1994 and 1996. Therefore, begin by walking students through the balance of payments, explaining how each of the transactions causes either a demand for or supply of a dollar.

CURRENT ACCOUNT

Balance Of Trade. When exports exceed imports, there is a balance of trade surplus, and the demand for dollars at the Bank of Reykjavik is higher than the supply of dollars. The United States ran a balance of trade surplus every year from the end of the Civil War through the early 1970s. We have had mixed results since then, but mostly we have had a balance of trade deficit (imports exceed exports, and more dollars are supplied at the Bank of Reykjavik than are demanded by foreigners.)

Interest and Dividend Payments. If a U.S. citizen holds foreign financial assets (such as a savings account in a foreign country), he or she earns interest or dividend payments paid in a foreign currency. The U.S. citizen probably does not want to hold that foreign currency, so he or she will take it to the Bank of Reykjavik to exchange it for dollars. That increases the SUPPLY of the foreign currency and the DEMAND for dollars. Likewise, if a foreigner owns a U.S. treasury bond (roughly 25% of privately held U.S. treasury debt is held by foreigners), and receives interest checks denominated in dollars, he or she will go to the Bank of Reykjavik and SUPPLY dollars and DEMAND foreign currency.

Transfers. When the U.S. gives foreign aid to a nation, it does so by supplying dollars to the country, which contributes to a deficit in the total balance of payments. Typically, the U.S. gives foreign aid and seldom, if ever, receives any in return. Thus, under the category of transfers there is nearly always a deficit as the U.S. supplies more dollars than are demanded by foreigners. At this point you can refer stu-

APPENDIX (continued)

dents to the 1991 balance of payments. In that year there was a surplus on the transfer account, meaning more dollars were demanded than supplied. This happened after the Gulf War, when Saudi Arabia, Kuwait and other countries repaid the U.S. for the money it spent in Operation Desert Storm.

Current Account Balance. All items discussed so far add up to the current account balance. Visuals 1 and 2 for this appendix show that the value of the current account balance has changed over time, as have the various components of the current account. From 1946 to 1970, the United States ran a trade surplus. Since 1971, the trade account has been in deficit every year since except 1973 and 1975. But even with this persistent trade deficit, interest payments on foreign investments have had sizable surpluses for the U.S., so that the current account realized a surplus from 1973-76 and 1980-81.

We can draw a line anywhere in the balance of payments account and sum items above the line. If we draw that line at the current account balance, all the entries below the line represent financing for the merchandise, services, investment income, and unilateral transfers (gifts), so the current account indicates whether a country is a net borrower from or a lender to the rest of the world. A current account surplus implies that a country is running a net deficit below the line, so that a country is a net lender to the rest of the world. In a period (year or quarter) during which a current account deficit is recorded, the country must borrow from abroad an amount sufficient to finance the deficit.

Since the balance of payments always balances, the large current account deficits that the U.S. experienced in the 1980s were matched by large capital account surpluses. The next section discusses the capital account and "settlement" accounts.

CAPITAL ACCOUNTS

Capital Flows. Capital flows include direct investment in the United States, foreign purchases of U.S. stocks and bonds, bank liabilities to foreigners, and official purchases of U.S. assets by foreign central banks. All of these transactions lead to a demand for dollars. If the current account is in deficit, that means that the U.S. is supplying more dollars in the international market than are being demanded for those transactions. Thus, the U.S. must borrow from abroad to finance that deficit. When the U.S. borrows by, say, selling a U.S. company's bond, foreigners pay for those bonds with dollars which they purchase from the Bank of Reykjavik. Thus, the supply of dollars caused by the current account deficit is offset by a demand for dollars as capital flows into the U.S. Of course, as we borrow from abroad it means that we must eventually pay back those borrowings. It was with some alarm in the early 1980s that the U.S. went from being the world's largest net lender abroad to the world's largest net borrower or debtor abroad. Some of this U.S. borrowing is from private foreign sources and some of it is from the monetary authorities of the various countries.

Official Purchases of U.S. and Foreign Financial Assets. This category is also referred to as the Official Settlements Balance. It is the value of the change in short-term capital held by foreign monetary agencies and official reserve asset transactions. Official institutions may not want to hold increasing stocks of dollars. If they sell the dollars, that increases the supply of dollars and drives the value of the dollar down. U.S. monetary authorities can buy up those dollars if they want to keep the value of the dollar high, but their ability to buy those dollars depends upon how much foreign currency reserves the Federal Reserve holds. If a country has run past surpluses and holds large amounts of foreign currencies, then it may be able to step in and prop up the value of its currency.

APPENDIX (continued)

On the other hand, if a country has a persistent current account deficit, it may have to go to the International Monetary Fund and borrow reserves if it does not want the value of its currency to fall in international markets. Often we read in the paper that the IMF has told some debtor country (Mexico or Brazil are recent examples), that it must tighten its money supply and stop running trade or government deficits. Students may wonder why the IMF can tell a country how to run its own monetary and fiscal policy. But, of course, if a country wants to borrow heavily from the IMF, it has to listen to what the IMF says. In the financial sections of large newspapers, you can often find reports on proclamations from the IMF about what some country must do. You can use that report to start a discussion in your class by asking your students how it is that an international agency can dictate policy to a country. If the students understand balance of payment accounts, they will be able to understand how that can happen.

VISUAL 1

The U.S. Balance of Payments Accounts for 1996

Demand for dollars (in millions)		Supply of dollars (in millions)		Net demand for dollars

Current Account

1) U.S. exports of goods and services	835,576	U.S. imports of goods and services	949,783	-114,207
2) Interest and dividends to U.S. holders of foreign financial assets	196,902	Interest and dividends to foreign holders of U.S. Financial assets	205,318	-8,416
3) Transfers (gifts, government grants)		Transfers (gifts, government grants)		-42,472
Total (current account				-165,095

Capital Account

4) Net private purchases of U.S. financial assets (capital inflow)	402,268	Net private purchases of foreign financial assets (capital outflow)	312,833	89,435
Totals (current and private capital accounts)				-75,660
Statistical discrepancy				-53,121
Totals (current and private capital accounts and statistical discrepancy)				-128,781
5) Net foreign official purchases of U.S. financial assets (capital inflow)	122,778	Net U.S. official purchases of foreign financial assets (capital outflow)	-6,003	128,781

VISUAL 2

The U.S. Balance of Payments Accounts for 1994

Demand for dollars (in millions)		Supply of dollars (in millions)		Net demand for dollars

Current Account

1) U.S. exports of goods and services	701,201	U.S. imports of goods and services	807,413	-106,212
2) Interest and dividends to U.S. holders of foreign financial assets	137,619	Interest and dividends to foreign holders of U.S. Financial assets	146,891	-9,272
3) Transfers (gifts, government grants)		Transfers (gifts, government grants)		-35,761
Total (current account				-151,245

Capital Account

4) Net private purchases of U.S. financial assets (capital inflow)	251,956	Net private purchases of foreign financial assets (capital outflow)	130,875	121,081
Totals (current and private capital accounts)				-30,164
Statistical discrepancy				-14,269
Totals (current and private capital accounts and statistical discrepancy)				-44,433
5) Net foreign official purchases of U.S. financial assets (capital inflow)	39,409	Net U.S. official purchases of foreign financial assets (capital outflow)	-5,024	44,433

ACTIVITY 1
INTERNATIONAL ECONOMIC TRENDS: INTERPRETING THE CURRENT ACCOUNT DEFICIT*

The trade deficit has been perceived as one of the more worrisome indicators of U.S. economic activity during the recent expansion. The current account the broadest measure of the nation's international trade positions reached a deficit of $165 billion in 1987. While this increase is often interpreted as evidence of a lack of "competitiveness" that could cause the United States to lose employment and wealth to other nations, there are reasons to be more sanguine about the U.S. international trade position.

First, although the current account deficit is near a record high in dollar terms it is far from its 1987 peak when expressed as a percentage of GDP. As the chart shows, the current account deficit amounted to about 2.2 percent of GDP in 1996, as compared to 3.6 percent in 1987. Although this deficit appears less foreboding relative to the size of the overall economy, it is still true that it is large by historical standards. How should this fact be interpreted? A basic accounting identity implies that there are two ways to evaluate the size of a current account deficit.

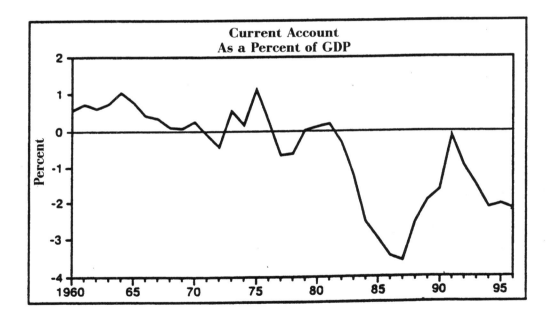

Current Account As a Percent of GDP

*Source: The Federal Reserve Bank of St. Louis.

ACTIVITY 1 (continued)

By definition, a deficit simply reflects an excess of imports over exports, and it is from this perspective that it is decried as indicating a lack of competitiveness or, sometimes, an unfair trading environment. However, as the excess of domestic spending over total production, the deficit can also be viewed as the net borrowing position of the United States. In general, a country that is running a current account deficit is borrowing from abroad to finance the acquisition of goods and services. When the current account is seen as a reflection of net borrowing, evaluation of the issue becomes a question of how the borrowed funds are being used.

Households that finance current consumption with debt, or firms that finance persistent operating losses through borrowing are clearly following a course that cannot be sustained indefinitely. However, if the borrowing is undertaken to purchase durable goods or productive equipment that will produce long-term payoffs in terms of future consumption, it can be reasonable. The situation of the current account deficit may be compared to that of individual households and firms, and the key question can be cast starkly as "does the deficit imply borrowing to finance a consumption binge, or does it indicate borrowing for productive use?"

While it is difficult to answer this question unambiguously, the evidence suggests that strong investment demand underlies the current economic expansion. Since the recession of 1990-91, real fixed investment spending has been growing at a rate of 6.9 percent, and consumer durables purchases have been rising at a 5.5 percent rate, compared to 2.6 percent growth of GDP. Moreover, spending for information technology has risen from 15 percent of total fixed investment to 24 percent over the same period. Only time will tell what the payoff to these investments will be, but they do give some reason to interpret the U.S. current account deficit with less apprehension.

FACTORS INFLUENCING BALANCE OF PAYMENTS

INTRODUCTION

In this lesson, students consider a variety of international economic activities, noting how each affects the balance of payments and the demand for and supply of dollars. This lesson is an extension of the material covered in Lesson 11, applying the ideas in that lesson to several "real world" activities and transactions.

CONCEPTS

Demand for dollars
Supply of dollars
Currency appreciation and depreciation

CONTENT STANDARDS

Voluntary exchange occurs only when all participating parties expect to gain. This is true for trade among individuals or organizations within a nation, and among individuals or organizations in different nations.

A nation pays for its imports with its exports.

Markets exist when buyers and sellers interact. This interaction determines market prices and thereby allocates scarce goods and services.

An exchange rate is the price of one nation's currency in terms of another nation's currency. Like other prices, exchange rates are determined by the forces of supply and demand. Foreign exchange markets allocate international currencies.

When the exchange rate between two currencies changes, the relative prices of the goods and services traded among countries using those currencies change; as a result, some groups gain and others lose.

OBJECTIVES

◆ Understand how different economic events influence the various components of the balance of payment.

◆ Explain shifts in the supply of or demand for dollars in response to different economic events.

◆ Understand the effects of domestic economic events on the international economy.

LESSON DESCRIPTION

Students read a list of various events and transactions. They determine how the events and transactions influence the balance of payments. By reference to Visuals 1 and 2 in Lesson 11, they determine how different transactions influence the demand for and the supply of dollars.

TIME REQUIRED

One class period.

MATERIALS

★ One transparency each of Visuals 1 and 2 from Lesson 11

★ One copy of Activity 1 for each student

★ A transparency or one copy of the answers to Activity 1 for each student (optional)

PROCEDURE

1. Give each student a copy of Activity 1.

2. Assign students to small groups; ask students in their groups to work through the various transactions.

3. Display either Visual 1 or 2 from Lesson 11 on the overhead so that the students have some basis for identifying the various segments of the balance of payments, but let them work through it on their own for about 15-20 minutes.

4. Display or pass out the answer sheet for Activity 1, or discuss students' answers to the questions.

ASSESSMENT

This lesson is critical for the students' subsequent work in Lesson 15. What the students should take out of this lesson is the idea that the demand for dollars is caused by exports and capital inflows and the supply of dollars is caused by imports and capital outflows. Interest and dividend payments are influenced by the outstanding stock of capital abroad or in the United States; they consequently change slowly are not immediately affected by changes in economic events. Thus, we do not include them as sources of demand for and supply of dollars.

For the assessment, draw a demand curve for dollars and a supply curve for dollars on the chalkboard or put it on an overhead transparency. Ask the students to label the sources of the demand for dollars (Exports and Capital Inflows) and the sources of the supply of dollars (Imports and Capital Inflows).

ACTIVITY 1

Transaction	Type of Activity (Use Category Numbers from Visuals 1 or 2 in Lesson 11)	Effect on Demand for and Supply of Dollars
A French business purchases machines from the United States		
A U.S. high school band visits Germany for the Oktoberfest		
People in Japan purchase bonds issued by General Motors		
The Unites States sends foreign aid To Ethiopia		
A U.S. citizen buys stock in British Leyland (a company with headquarters in the UK)		
A U.S. citizen cashes a dividend check issued by British Leyland		
The U.S. Federal Reserve Bank uses Japanese yen to buy dollars in the currency market		
The U.S. limits the number of Japanese cars that can be imported in the U.S.		
Fearing inflation in their countries, Foreigners buy U.S. treasury bonds as investments		
The U.S. Treasury pays interest to holders of bonds in other countries		
After Operation Desert Storm, Saudi Arabia and Kuwait make payments to the U.S. military		

ACTIVITY 1
ANSWERS

Transaction	Type of Activity (Use Category Numbers from Visuals 1 or 2 in Lesson 11)	Effect on Demand for and Supply of Dollars
A French business purchases machines from the United States	1 - Export	Demand for $
A U.S. high school band visits Germany for the Oktoberfest	1 - Import	Supply of $
People in Japan purchase bonds issued by General Motors	4 - Capital inflow	Demand for $
The Unites States sends foreign aid To Ethiopia	3 - Transfer	Supply of $
A U.S. citizen buys stock in British Leyland (a company with headquarters in the UK)	4 - Capital outflow	Supply of $
A U.S. citizen cashes a dividend check issued by British Leyland	2 - Interest to U.S.	Demand for $
The U.S. Federal Reserve Bank uses Japanese yen to buy dollars in the currency market	5 - Official Transaction	Demand for $
The U.S. limits the number of Japanese cars that can be imported in the U.S.	1 - Decrease Imports	Supply of $
Fearing inflation in their countries, Foreigners buy U.S. treasury bonds as investments	4 - Capital inflow	Demand for $
The U.S. Treasury pays interest to holders of bonds in other countries	2 - Interest	Supply of $
After Operation Desert Storm, Saudi Arabia and Kuwait make payments to the U.S. military	3 - Transfer	Demand for $

From *Focus: International Economics*, © National Council on Economic Education. New York. NY.

WHERE TO BUILD A FACTORY

INTRODUCTION

Companies from many countries often buy or build factories in other countries in order to reduce production costs and distribute their products more efficiently. Just as we see U.S. companies locating plants in certain areas within the U.S. to reduce transportation costs and to better facilitate distribution to the rest of the country, we now see multinational companies locating plants around the world in order to serve foreign markets more efficiently. This lesson explores the factors that influence decisions about where to locate a factory.

CONCEPTS

Production costs
Demand
Markets
Profits

CONTENT STANDARDS

Effective decision-making requires comparing the additional costs of alternatives with the additional benefits. Most choices involve doing a little more or a little less of something; few choices are all-or-nothing decisions.

Investment in factories, machinery, new technology, and the health, education, and training of people can raise future standards of living.

Institutions evolve in market economies to help individuals and groups accomplish their goals. Banks, labor unions, corporations, legal systems, and not-for-profit organizations are examples of important institutions. A different kind of institution, clearly defined and well enforced property rights, is essential to a market economy.

OBJECTIVES

◆ Determine the factors that influence decisions on where to build a factory.

LESSON DESCRIPTION

Through discussion in small groups and reports to the full class, students evaluate the factors that influence decisions about where to invest abroad.

TIME REQUIRED

Two class periods. Day one for procedures 1 through 7 and class discussions, plus additional research on one or more countries as a homework assignment. Day two for the Assessment.

MATERIALS

★ One copy of Activity 1 and Activity 2 for each student.

PROCEDURE

1. Divide the class into groups of 4-6 students.

2. Distribute a copy of Activity 1 to each student. Have the students read the Activity. Remind the students that they want to build an *automotive* factory.

   A. Have each group of students answer the following questions about factors that influence decisions about where to build a factory.

   B. Have one student from each group report the group's answers with the class; discuss any differences in the groups' answers.

   C. Ask the students how their answers might change if they were not building an automotive factory, but rather some other kind of factory. For instance, ask them how their answers would change if they were building a computer factory or a toy factory.

3. Distribute a copy of Activity 2 to each student. The handout presents basic economic information about five countries: the U.S., Germany, China, Brazil, and India.

4. Have students read the information provided and use it to evaluate the advantages and

disadvantages of locating an automobile assembly plant in each of these countries. Students should also be encouraged to use almanacs, encyclopedias, magazine articles, and other sources of information in the classroom or library to obtain additional information for making their decision. *(You may want to make this a homework assignment prior to the day of discussion.)*

5. Each group of students should decide which country to recommend as the site of the assembly plant.

6. Ask each group to report its decision to the class and the reasons for it.

7. Have each group discuss the global implications of the decision it reached. Some questions that can be used to guide the discussion are as follows:

A. What countries would be affected by this decision?

B. What will be the effects of this decision be on:

1) Workers in different countries?

2) Consumers in different countries?

3) The multinational corporation's stockholders?

4) The governments of different countries?

C. How will your decision to build a factory in the country you chose link that country's economy more closely to the rest of the world? *(Each group's answers will vary depending on the country it selected. However, from these questions students should begin to see how the rise of international trade and multinational corporations has led to increasing global interdependence. Economic decisions made daily by managers of large corporations have global effects on workers, consumers, stockholders, and national governments. Increasingly, the various countries of the world are linked in a global economy.)*

ASSESSMENT
When the students have completed Activity 1 and 2, have them choose a country (one other than those used in Activity 2) and defend that country as the best country to locate an apparel factory. In defending the country they choose, have students present current data gathered from the library, magazines, Internet, etc., to support their position.

ACTIVITY 1
WHERE TO BUILD A FACTORY

In today's global economy, many firms try to reduce production costs and sell their products in other countries more efficiently by building factories abroad. In Activity 2, you will choose a country in which to build an automotive factory. In this activity, you will consider some of the key factors that are important in making decisions about where to build the factory:

1. **Wages.** How much do factory workers get paid in each country? Wages are a key cost of production in this kind of a factory.

2. **Availability of skilled labor.** How good is the education system in the county? Will it be easy to obtain enough experienced and educated workers to fill positions for engineers, mechanics, accountants, managers?

3. **Political stability.** How stable is the country's government? Will it be able to maintain law and order? To protect your investment, you will only want to build a factory in a country where you are reasonably sure that you can continue to operate the factory for years in the future. A major concern for many multinational corporations with plants in some developing countries is that a revolutionary government may come to power and take over (nationalize) one of their factories. A commitment to well-defined property rights is therefore important.

4. **Transportation and communications systems.** How well is the country linked to the rest of the world? This measure not only considers the transportation and communication technologies in a country; it also considers the geographic location of the country compared to potential trading partners. Will you be able to ship in parts and ship out the finished products quickly and cheaply? Ideally, the factory should be located either near the world's leading markets or where there is a strong chance to establish strategic positions in markets expected to grow rapidly in the future. Availability of raw materials is important; you may want to locate close to the source of supply.

5. **Import/export restrictions.** Are there any tariffs, import quotas, or other trade barriers that will make importing or exporting either more or less expensive? Where there are tariffs and quotas, importing and exporting will be more costly. Between countries participating in free trade agreements, trade will be cheaper.

6. **Government regulation.** Before deciding to invest in a factory, a company wants to know such things as: What government regulations will you have to comply with? Will excessive red tape interfere with your company's ability to do business? How much will you have to pay in taxes? etc.

7. **Cultural and linguistic factors.** Will language differences create communication problems? Will the nation's customs be compatible with the established principles and procedures of your company? Local attitudes and practices that determine the relationship between labor and management will be especially important.

8. **Size of the foreign country's/region's market.** The size of the potential market for your good should be considered in deciding where to build your factory. If you can sell more of your finished goods in one country versus another, other things being equal, you might want to consider the country with the larger market.

9. **Questions.** In your group, discuss and arrive at an answer for each of the following questions:

- Which of these eight factors is most important? Why?

ACTIVITY 1 (continued)

- Which is least important? Why?

- Are there any other important factors that
  are not listed above?

- Rank the eight factors from most important
  (#1) to least important (#8)

_____ Wages

_____ Availability of skilled labor

_____ Political stability

_____ Transportation system

_____ Import/export restrictions

_____ Government regulation

_____ Cultural and linguistic factors

_____ Size of the foreign
            country's/region's market

ACTIVITY 2
WHERE TO BUILD A FACTORY

Before deciding where to build a factory in another country, people who own and manage a company must gather information about the different nations where the factory might be built. Provided here is basic information on six countries that are being considered by a multinational automobile company as a potential location for a large automobile assembly plant. Use this information and any other information about these countries that you can find in magazines, newspapers, and encyclopedias, etc. Your group must decide in which of these countries the plant should be built. Each group will be asked to report on its decision and to explain how that decision was made. (The analysis of each country highlights important economic factors as they existed late in 1997. You may want your students to update this information.)

The United States
The American unemployment rate is low, around 5-6%. Among those employed, there is a large body of skilled labor. American skilled labor is among the highest-paid in the world. The average hourly wage for production and manufacturing labor is $17.44. Also, most autoworkers are members of the United Autoworkers (UAW), a labor union where the relationship between labor and management has been adversarial. Facing intense competition from Japan and other foreign auto companies, some U.S. firms have tried to develop more cooperative relationships.

Some foreign automobile companies such as Nissan, Toyota, and Honda have U.S. plants where workers are not unionized.

The political structure in the U.S. is extremely stable, with a strong democratic tradition. The last major internal conflict was the Civil War in 1860s. The transition from one national leader to the next is calm and peaceful. There is very little chance that the U.S. government

will be overthrown by a revolution. Government regulations have hurt the auto industry in the past, however. With strict antitrust laws, cooperation between rival firms has been nearly nonexistent. There are also many regulations in factories dealing with labor safety, pollution control, and employment practices.

The U.S. market for automobiles is one of the largest in the world. Producing in the U.S. to serve the American market has become popular in recent decades, especially in periods when the dollar has been weak against foreign currency. This makes it cheaper to produce within the U.S. as opposed to producing in another country and exporting to the U.S. market. The U.S. does have a well-established transportation and communication infrastructure, which would facilitate trade not only within the U.S. but also to its neighbors and the rest of the world

Germany
Germany is a well-educated society with a large pool of skilled labor. The unemployment rate in the western part of Germany is about 11%; in the eastern part it is about 15%. Even though the unemployment rate is high, German labor costs are very high. The hourly wage for production and manufacturing labor is $31.87.

The German political situation is stable, but in reunifying East and West Germany political leaders have been given the difficult task of bringing the former East Germany up to Western German living standards. This has caused a financial drain for the government because of the investments needed to create a modern infrastructure and to provide social services in the East. The Germans have spent the equivalent of several billion U.S. dollars in this process. Although it has been costly, the East German economy has enjoyed 8% annual growth since 1991. The German government does pro-

---

ACTIVITY 2 (continued)

vide tax breaks to firms that locate in Eastern Germany.

Germany shares its borders with many large European countries. It is well positioned to export goods to the former Soviet bloc nations. Germany is a member of the European Union, which makes trading within the EU less costly. However, there are other EU countries in which one could build a plant where labor would be half as costly as the German labor, but less productive.

China

China's population is the largest in the world, with over 1.2 billion people. Literacy is a large problem. There is a large rural sector in China of about 100 million people who currently work only part-time. The relationship between firms and workers is generally good.

The atmosphere for business in China differs from the atmosphere found in more modern countries. First, there is a large government sector to contend with. There is a lot of red tape and corruption. Extortion and bribery are more common in China than in most Western nations.

In a global economy where one may want to have access to the east, it is imperative to realize that there are tensions between China and Korea, China and Taiwan, and China and Australia. There is, however, close access to the entire Asian region. China can trade with the Far East, but it can also reach Russia, the former Soviet nations, and Southeast Asia.

With the return of Hong Kong to China in 1997, China's political leaders vowed that they would continue to move from a centrally-planned economy to a more open and market-based economy. Political change is still slow, however, with protests such as the student uprisings in Tienamen square having a lingering effect on the country.

Even with recent reforms, there is still a dominant presence of key state-run industries. But as China has accepted the move towards a market-based economy, China's GDP has tripled since 1978. It is one of the biggest countries for direct foreign investment.

The market in China is still emerging. There may not be a large demand for goods like automobiles today. However, given its size and population, once the Chinese market is developed it will be extremely large and demand conditions will change for the better.

Brazil

Brazil is the largest country in South America in terms of population and area. The population in the mid-1990s was approximately 160 million. It borders almost all South American countries. Also, Brazil is a member of Mercosur, which is a customs union made up of Argentina, Brazil, Paraguay, and Uruguay. Brazil's location and involvement in Mercosur make it an important gateway to other South American nations. This is especially important because recent market studies of the area encompassed by the customs union show a large emerging market for automobiles.

The Brazilian government is trying to encourage direct foreign investment. It has liberalized trade policy to welcome foreign investors. Also, Brazil has a large base of technology, and the government plans to strengthen its transportation and communication infrastructure.

Although the Brazilian economy has had problems in the past with hyperinflation, the government believes it has rising prices under control. In 1994 consumer prices rose 2000%, but in 1995 they only rose 23%. Although prices are becoming stable, high inflation has led to debt problems in Brazil. There are also serious literacy and poverty problems in the country.

ACTIVITY 2 (continued)

India

The population of India is close to a billion. The middle class population is over 200 million, making India an emerging market with strong potential. The U.S. is its largest trading partner, but countries like Japan and Korea are trying to increase their share of India's foreign trade. India has a large supply of skilled labor, but workers in India have been prone to strike in the past. The caste system leads to social struggles. India also has a tenuous and volatile relationship with Pakistan. Both of these nations have nuclear capabilities.

India has a well-established legal and commercial code, similar to English common law, which makes doing business relatively easy. The government is trying to reduce the amount of red tape involved in foreign business. Licenses are now easier to get than before. India has lowered tariffs from a maximum of 300% to 50%. Access to potential trading partners is good India is close to South East Asian markets and Chinese markets, as well as markets which use Indian Ocean trade routes.

Unlike other emerging countries, India has managed to privatize major industries including the power, aviation, and telephone industries. However, slow improvement in telephone service is a major problem in India's quest to become a participant in the global economy. Three out of four villages do not have telephone service at all. In villages with telephone service, there is often little or no access to long distance service. India also has a serious problem with poverty and disease.

FOREIGN EXCHANGE RATES

INTRODUCTION

Students often hear or read news reports about foreign exchange rates. Students who have traveled in other countries or whose families have recently moved to the United States probably have personal experience with exchange rates, and they may be curious about factors underlying the value of their currency exchanges. Without some formal instruction on this topic, however, it is difficult to understand many of these news items. This lesson introduces students to basic information about exchange rates.

CONCEPTS

Foreign exchange rates
Fixed exchange rates
Floating exchange rates
Currency appreciation
Currency depreciation

CONTENT STANDARDS

Markets exist whenever buyers and sellers interact. This interaction determines market prices and thereby allocates scarce goods and services.

An exchange rate is the price of one nation's currency in terms of another nation's currency. Like other prices, exchange rates are determined by the forces of supply and demand. Foreign exchange markets allocate international currencies.

When the exchange rate between two currencies changes, the relative prices of the goods and services traded among countries using those currencies change; as a result, some groups gain and others lose.

OBJECTIVES

◆ Explain why people want currency from other countries.

◆ Identify where to find information about current exchange rates.
◆ Be able to read exchange rate tables in newspapers.
◆ Define "fixed exchange rates" and "floating exchange rates."
◆ Explain the difference below a strong dollar and a weak dollar, and explain who would benefit from each.

LESSON DESCRIPTION

Students are shown various newspaper headlines referring to the value of the dollar in foreign exchange markets. They learn what exchange rates are, and they participate in a simulation where they discover answers to 10 frequently-asked questions about foreign exchange rates.

TIME REQUIRED

One class period.

MATERIALS

★ One transparency each of Visuals 1 and 2
★ One copy of Activity 1, cut apart for every 10 students. The activity is divided into 10 sections, and each student should be given one section.
★ One copy of Activity 2 for each student.
★ **Optional**: One copy of Activity 1 for each student, to use for study and review after the activity is completed.

PROCEDURE

1. Display Visual 1. Ask the students if they have seen newspaper headlines like these or heard announcements like these on the news. Read one of the headlines (for example "Dollar is Expected to Gain This Week") and ask students to speculate about what this means. *(Students have probably seen such headlines or heard similar statements in news broadcasts. It is likely that many will not know what the headlines mean. All of the headlines refer to the value of the dollar in foreign exchange markets. When the dollar gains ["advances," "surges"], it purchases more foreign currency than before. When the dollar falls ["sags," "declines"], it purchases less foreign currency than before. [Some*

students may speculate that the headlines refer to inflation. Tell them that this was a good guess. Since inflation means that prices on average are rising, and the dollar buys less, the value of the dollar in international markets does decline owing to inflation. However, the expressions on the transparency generally refer to the value of the dollar in foreign exchange markets.]) You may wish to bring in recent newspaper articles or headlines on this topic to show to students, along with Visual 1. *The Wall Street Journal* lists "Foreign Exchange" daily under the "Today's Contents" section on page one, and it is a good source.

2. Display Visual 2, keeping the portion below the horizontal line covered with a piece of paper so that the answer to the question is not visible. Read the transparency to the students, and ask them to answer the question about the exchange rate for the Japanese yen. Read the answer at the bottom of the transparency.

Optional: Some students will be able to convert currencies quickly, whereas others may have trouble doing so. If you wish to give a formula for currency conversion, try explaining the examples this way:

If $1 = 100 yen, how many dollars (or what fraction of a dollar) equals one yen? To have "one yen" in the equation, you need to divide each side of the equation by 100, so that 1/100 dollar, or 1¢ = 100/100 yen, or 1 yen

Likewise, if $1 = 5 francs, to find out how many dollars (or what fraction of a dollar) equals 1 franc, divide each side of the equation by 5, so that 1/5 dollar, or 20¢ = 5/5 francs, or one franc.

3. Announce the following: "You will now participate in an activity where you will learn answers to 10 frequently-asked questions relating to foreign exchange rates. First, you will each become knowledgeable about one topic on exchange rates so you can serve as a consultant on one of the 10 questions."

Divide the class into 10 small groups. Give students in each group copies of one of the sections of Activity 1. Assign each group to be a consultant on one of the topics. Give groups about 10 minutes to read the papers and discuss the information with each other. Tell them to make sure that everyone in the group understands the information they are given and is prepared to explain it to others in the class. *(In classes with students of mixed ability, try to have at least one strong student in each group.)*

4. Distribute a copy of Activity 2 to each student. Read the directions at the top of the page to the class and ask if there are any questions. Also explain that:

A. Students do not need to stay in their groups during the activity.

B. Consultants need to figure out which question they can answer. Question numbers are not provided.

C. Students must discuss the questions with a consultant; they should not simply copy someone's paper.

D. If some students finish answering the 10 questions before the others have finished, they should volunteer to help others with the question for which they are the consultant. No one is finished until he or she has answered all 10 questions and everyone in the class has the answer to the question for which he or she is the consultant.

5. Tell students to begin the activity. They will need to leave their seats and circulate around the room. *(You may want to begin the activity by demonstrating the search process. For example, take a copy of Activity 2 from a student, and say, "I need to find out what a fixed exchange rate is — Question #3. Who is a consultant on this?" When the appropriate consultants respond, tell students that they should talk with one of the consultants to discuss the answer to the question. When they understand the answer, the fixed-exchange rate consultant*

should initial their paper next to number 3. They could then offer to help that person with the question for which they are a consultant.)

6. Stop the activity when all or almost all the students have finished. Begin the class discussion by asking, "From the information provided in this activity, why is it important to know about exchange rates?" *(Many answers are possible. Students may respond that the information will help people to understand what is going on in the news, will help foreign travelers, investors, and businesses that import and export, etc.)*

Next discuss each question on Activity 2. Call on students who were not the consultants for that question. *(You may use Activity 1 as a guide to the answers. Students should add to their written answers and make corrections on Activity 2 during the discussion.)*

7. **Optional:** If you made copies of Activity 1 for each student, distribute them after the discussion in Procedure 6. Students may read through the handout to reinforce their understanding of the concepts.

ASSESSMENT

To review this activity, ask each student to use information from this lesson to write a question that could be given on a test. The question could be multiple choice, short-answer, a definition, fill-in-the-blank, true-false, etc. Call on a student to read his or her question to the class, and have that student choose another student to answer the question. The student who answers the question then reads his or her question and chooses someone to answer it, and so on. Collect the questions, and use some of them on a test covering this material.

Dollar Surges

Dollar's Decline Presents Dilemma

Dollar Is Expected to Gain This Week

Dollar Plunges

Dollar Sags

Dollar Advances

Dollar Skids

Dollar Posts Moderate Gains

Dollar Falls

U.S. Dollar Goes on Rebound

Dollar Sags to 4-Month Low

Dollar Edges Up

Dollar Receives Pummeling

WHAT IS AN EXCHANGE RATE?

An exchange rate is the amount of one country's currency that is equal to one unit of another country's currency.

Exchange rates can be expressed two ways. For example, if one U.S. dollar equals two Dutch Guilders, the exchange rate is 2 guilders per dollar, or 1/2 dollar per guilder.

If one dollar is equal to 5 French francs, the exchange rate is 5 francs per dollar, or 20¢ (1/5 dollar) per franc.

Figure this one out yourself: You want to exchange dollars for Japanese yen. Your bank gives you 100 yen for each dollar.

State the exchange rate in two ways.*

1._____

2. _____

_____

*Answer: The exchange rate is 100 yen per dollar, or 1¢ (1/100 dollar) per yen.

ACTIVITY 1
EXPERTS ON INTERNATIONAL TRADE

You are a consultant on why people in one country want currency from another country.

People exchange their country's currency for another country's currency for many reasons. International trade requires using money from different countries. For example, suppose a California company sells microchips to Japan. The Japanese have yen to spend, but the Americans want to end up with dollars. And a Japanese company that sells television sets to the U.S. wants to end up with yen, not dollars. Somewhere along the way, dollars have to be exchanged for yen. People traveling to other countries also use foreign currencies. People who buy stocks or bonds in a foreign country use that country's currency to pay for the stocks or bonds. Some people buy and sell foreign currency for speculative reasons. This means that they try to make profits by buying at a lower price and selling at a higher price.

You are a consultant on where to find information about current exchange rates, and how to read newspaper exchange-rate tables.

Most major newspapers publish charts every day giving exchange rates for the U.S. dollar and other currencies. This information is usually found in the business section of the paper. Other sources of information include the Internet, banks, and other financial institutions. Here is a copy of a chart from the *Wall Street Journal* (June 12, 1997). The column labeled **Dollar** tells you how much foreign currency could be purchased with one dollar on that day. For example, one dollar bought about 1.4 Swiss francs, or about 62% of a pound from the United Kingdom. The other columns tell how much foreign currency could have been purchased with one unit of money from other countries. For example, look at the column for German marks (D-Marks, standing for Deutsche marks). One mark purchased about 80% of a Canadian dollar, about 58% of a U.S. dollar, or about 982 Italian lira. (Note: these exchange rates apply to trading among banks in amounts of $1 million or more. People trading less money would generally receive less foreign currency per dollar.)

	Dollar	Pound	Sfranc	Guilder	Peso	Yen	Lira	D-Mark	Ffranc	CdnDlr
Key Currency Cross Rates Late New York Trading, June 12, 1997										
Canada	1.3841	2.2589	.95885	.71134	.17386	.01212	.00082	.80029	.23721	....
France	5.8350	9.5227	4.0423	3.0009	.73295	.05108	.00344	3.3738	....	4.2157
Germany	1.7295	2.8225	1.1981	.88948	.21725	.01514	.00102	....	.29640	1.2495
Italy	1698.0	2771.1	1176.3	873.28	213.29	14.865	....	981.79	291.0	1226.8
Japan	114.23	186.42	79.134	58.748	14.349	....	.06727	66.048	19,577	82.53
Mexico	7.9610	12.992	5.5151	4.0943	....	.06969	.00469	4.6031	1.3644	5.7518
Netherlands	1.9444	3.3733	1.3470	....	.24424	.01702	.00115	1.1243	.33323	1.4048
Switzerland	1.4435	2.3558	....	.74239	.18132	.01264	.00085	.83463	.24739	1.0429
U.K.	.61275	....	.42449	.31513	.07697	..00536	.00036	.35429	.10501	.44270
U.S.	....	1.6320	.69276	.51430	.12561	.00875	.00059	.57820	.17138	.72249

Source: Dow Jones

From *Focus: International Economics*, © National Council on Economic Education, New York. NY.

ACTIVITY 1 (continued)

You are a consultant on fixed exchange rates.

In countries that have fixed exchange rates, one country's money may be exchanged for a set amount of another country's money. The rates change only if the government decides to change the fixed rate. Between 1945 and 1973, most of the world's major economies had fixed exchange rates. For example, $1.00 was worth 4 West German Deutsche marks, or 4.90 French francs. Most major economies today, including the U.S., no longer have fixed exchange rate systems. Notable exceptions include West European countries making up the European Union (EU), most of which have fixed exchange rates with each other. Also, many Latin American countries fix (or peg) their exchange rates to the U.S. dollar. Exchange rates cannot be fixed forever, so even countries that fix or peg their exchange rates change the fixed rate or let them float from time to time.

An advantage of having fixed exchange rates is that they are stable. Business people, travelers, and others know how much foreign money a dollar will buy, which makes it easier to plan for the future. A disadvantage is that a fixed exchange rate may not accurately reflect what people are really willing to pay for the foreign currency. Shortages or surpluses of the currencies may occur, leading governments to intervene with large changes in the fixed exchange rates.

You are a consultant on floating exchange rates.

The terms "floating" and "flexible" exchange rates mean the same thing. Today, most of the world's major economies, including the United States, have some form of a floating (or flexible) exchange rate system. In countries with floating exchange rates, the amount of one country's money that may be exchanged for another country's money is determined primarily by the supply of and demand for the different currencies. For example, if foreigners demand a lot more dollars (perhaps to travel in the United States), the value of the dollar goes up, and the dollar then would buy relatively more foreign currency. If Americans supply a lot more dollars (for example, because they want to buy more foreign currency to travel abroad), the value of the dollar goes down, and the dollar then would buy relatively less foreign currency. In a completely free-floating system, governments would not be involved in this process at all, but this is seldom the case. Governments frequently intervene in foreign exchange markets to prevent wide fluctuations and to try to keep exchange rates within certain desired ranges. An advantage of floating exchange rates is that the value of a currency changes as supply and demand conditions for the currency change. A disadvantage is that some flexible exchange rates are extremely unstable, making it difficult for people who need foreign currency to estimate how much it will cost.

You are a consultant on whether the exchange rate for the dollar changes often.

Exchange rates for the U.S. dollar change constantly. Exchange rates often vary considerably over years, months, weeks, and even during a given day. For example, between 1979 and 1985, the dollar rose an average of 80% against other major currencies. Then, from 1985 through 1991, the dollar fell against other major currencies by about the same amount. During the week from May 5 to May 9, 1997, the dollar fell 5% against the Japanese yen. And the dollar bought 3 more Italian lira at 4 p.m. on Tuesday July 1, 1997 than at 4 p.m. the day before (1701 lira per dollar compared to 1698 lira). These changing rates affect prices of imports, exports, and related goods, and they affect the costs and profits of businesses engaged in international trade.

ACTIVITY 1 (continued)

You are a consultant on the role of gold in foreign exchange transactions.

Gold no longer has an official role in foreign exchange transactions, and the U.S. dollar is no longer backed by a certain amount of gold. Before 1971, the value of the dollar was defined to be a fixed amount of gold (1/35 of an ounce), and foreign central banks holding dollars could exchange the dollars for gold. For example, if the French central bank received $350 from a French winery that had earned the dollars by exporting wine to the United States, the French central bank was entitled to exchange the dollars for 10 ounces of gold from the U.S. government. We no longer operate on this gold standard. People who hold dollars today are not entitled to turn them in for a commodity such as gold or silver. The dollar is backed only by the strength of the U.S. economy and the fact that people are willing to accept it in payment because they can use it to buy goods and services produced in the U.S.

You are a consultant on what is meant by a "strong" dollar.

A strong dollar means that the dollar is currently exchanging for more foreign currency than it did in the past. For example, if the dollar is worth 120 yen today, and was only worth 100 yen last year, the dollar is stronger today than last year. A strong dollar makes imports cheaper for Americans, since it takes fewer dollars to buy the foreign currency necessary to buy a foreign product. Suppose a certain radio cost 10,000 yen in Japan, both last year and this year. According to the example above, last year an American would have had to pay $100 to get enough yen to buy the radio. This year an American would only have had to pay about $83 to get enough yen to buy the radio. The radio hasn't changed, and the price of the radio in Japan hasn't changed. But since the exchange rate changed and the dollar is stronger, the radio is cheaper for Americans. At the same time, American goods would become more expensive for the Japanese to buy, since it would take more yen to buy a dollar.

You are a consultant on what is meant by a "weak" dollar.

A weak dollar means that the dollar is currently exchanging for less foreign currency than it did in the past. For example, if the dollar is worth 4 German marks today, but was worth 5 marks last year, the dollar is weaker against the mark today than last year. German products would be more expensive for Americans to buy today compared to last year, because it would take more dollars to pay for them. Suppose some binoculars made in Germany cost 500 marks, both last year and this year. Last year you could have exchanged $100 to get enough marks to buy the binoculars. This year you would need to exchange $125 to get enough marks to buy the binoculars. The binoculars haven't changed, and their price in Germany hasn't changed. They are more expensive to Americans because the exchange rate changed and made the dollar weaker. At the same time, American goods would become cheaper for the Germans to buy, since it would take fewer marks to buy a dollar.

You are a consultant on how some Americans benefit from a strong dollar.

When the dollar becomes stronger in foreign exchange markets, many Americans benefit. American consumers who buy imports benefit, and that includes most people in the U.S. A strong dollar means that dollars can be exchanged for more foreign currency than before, so it is cheaper for American consumers to purchase imported goods. Americans who work in businesses that

From *Focus: International Economics*. © National Council on Economic Education, New York, NY.

ACTIVITY 1 (continued)

import goods also benefit, since U.S. consumers will buy more of the products they import. A stronger dollar means that it becomes cheaper for American tourists and business people to travel abroad. The reverse is true for a weak dollar; when the dollar is weak, it is more expensive to travel abroad and imports are more expensive.

You are a consultant on how some Americans are hurt by a strong dollar.

When the dollar becomes stronger in foreign exchange markets, some Americans are hurt. Since a strong dollar makes imports relatively cheaper, Americans who sell products that compete with foreign imports may lose sales. For example, if Japanese cars are cheaper because the dollar is stronger, people may buy more Japanese cars and fewer American cars. This would hurt the American automobile industry. Also, when the dollar is strong relative to foreign currencies, U.S. exports become more expensive for foreigners to buy. American businesses that export goods abroad may lose business. This also makes the U.S. trade deficit worse. (A country has a trade deficit if it imports more goods than it exports.)

ACTIVITY 2
TEN QUESTIONS ON FOREIGN EXCHANGE RATES

Directions: In your work on Activity 1, you developed an answer to one of the following questions. That makes you a consultant on that question for this activity. Other students in class are consultants on the other questions. Answer all the questions below by locating consultants and asking them to explain the answers to you. Your classmates will also consult you for help on your question.

Once you locate a consultant for a question, or when someone asks you for help on your subject, discuss the answers with each other to make sure you understand them. Then write the answers (on your own paper) in the space provided.

You do not have to answer the questions in the order in which they are written on this paper.

You must talk with at least nine different consultants one for each question other than your own. Have all the consultants you talk to write their initials in the space provided before each question after you are satisfied that you understand the answer to that question. Write your initials in the space provided on your classmates' papers when they understand the explanations you give to them.

_____ 1. Why would people in one country want another country's currency? Give at least three reasons.

_____ 2. (A) Where can you find information about what exchange rates are today?

(B) What is the exchange rate between U.S. dollars and Mexican pesos shown in the following table?

	Dollar	Pound	Sfranc	Guilder	Peso	Yen	Lira	D-Mark	Ffranc	CdnDir
	Key Currency Cross Rates Late New York Trading, June 12, 1997									
Canada	1.3841	2.2589	.95885	.71134	.17386	.01212	.00082	.80029	.23721	....
France	5.8350	9.5227	4.0423	3.0009	.73295	.05108	.00344	3.3738	....	4.2157
Germany	1.7295	2.8225	1.1981	.88948	.21725	.01514	.00102	....	.29640	1.2495
Italy	1698.0	2771.1	1176.3	873.28	213.29	14.865	....	981.79	291.0	1226.8
Japan	114.23	186.42	79.134	58.748	14.349	....	.06727	66.048	19.577	82.53
Mexico	7.9610	12.992	5.5151	4.0943	....	.06969	.00469	4.6031	1.3644	5.7518
Netherlands	1.9444	3.3733	1.3470	....	.24424	.01702	.00115	1.1243	.33323	1.4048
Switzerland	1.4435	2.3558	....	.74239	.18132	.01264	.00085	.83463	.24739	1.0429
U.K.	.61275	....	.42449	.31513	.07697	..00536	.00036	.35429	.10501	.44270
U.S.	....	1.6320	.69276	.51430	.12561	.00875	.00059	.57820	.17138	.72249

Source: Dow Jones

From *Focus: International Economics*, © National Council on Economic Education, New York, NY.

ACTIVITY 2 (continued)

_____ 3. What is a fixed exchange rate? Explain.

_____ 4. What is a floating (or flexible) exchange rate? Explain.

_____ 5. Does the exchange rate for the dollar change very often? Explain.

_____ 6. What is the role of gold in foreign exchange transactions? Is the dollar backed by a fixed amount of gold?

_____ 7. What does it mean when the dollar is "strong"? Explain.

_____ 8. What does it mean when the dollar is "weak"? Explain.

_____ 9. Give examples of Americans who would benefit from a strong dollar.

_____ 10. Give examples of Americans who would be hurt by a strong dollar.

FOREIGN CURRENCY AND FOREIGN EXCHANGE

INTRODUCTION

This lesson also deals with exchange rates. It presents the factors that lead to changes in the value of currencies. Problems involved in trying to fix a currency's value are also explained. The lesson gets somewhat technical, so be sure your students have completed earlier lessons on exchange rates or have the necessary background from other sources.

At the end of World War II, many of the industrialized countries of the world formed the International Monetary Fund and established an arrangement that determined exchange rates for nearly 30 years. That agreement, known as the Bretton Woods agreement, had all countries tie the value of their currency to gold. By doing that, the countries also linked the values for their currencies together. For example, the United States set the value of the dollar at $35 per ounce of gold. Great Britain set the value of the pound at 12.5 pounds per ounce of gold. Given those two rates, the exchange rate for dollars and pounds was set at $2.80 per pound. That rate held from 1948 until 1967, when the pound was "devalued."

More generally, it became increasingly difficult for governments to defend fixed exchange rates in the 1960s. In 1971 President Nixon decided that the United States would no longer exchange gold for dollars. By 1973, the Bretton Woods system of fixed exchange rates collapsed.

Each country is now free to set its own policy toward its exchange rate, and many countries have chosen floating or flexible rates in which exchange rate values rise and fall freely as their value is determined in world currency markets. Although the world generally operates under a system of floating exchange rates, there have been some cases in recent years (e.g., in the European Union) where countries or groups of countries have attempted to fix or peg their exchange rates. This situation is sometimes referred to as a "dirty float."

CONCEPTS

Floating exchange rates
Managed exchange rates
Devaluation and appreciation
Currency price floors

CONTENT STANDARDS

Markets exist when buyers and sellers interact. This interaction determines market prices and thereby allocates scarce goods and services.

An exchange rate is the price of one nation's currency in terms of another nation's currency. Like other prices, exchange rates are determined by the forces of supply and demand. Foreign exchange markets allocate international currencies.

When the exchange rate between two currencies changes, the relative prices of the goods and services traded among countries using those currencies change; as a result, some groups gain and others lose.

Prices send signals and provide incentives to buyers and sellers. When supply or demand changes, market prices adjust, affecting incentives.

Government-enforced price ceilings set below the market clearing price and government-enforced price floors set above the market clearing price distort price signals and incentives to producers and consumers. Price ceilings cause persistent shortages, while price floors cause persistent surpluses.

OBJECTIVES

◆ Understand what it means for a currency to appreciate or depreciate.
◆ Be able to give examples of economic events that will change the value of a currency.
◆ Explain the difficulties involved in trying to maintain an exchange rate for a currency

apart from its market value.

◆ Identify different groups in a country that will favor or oppose appreciation or depreciation in the value of their nation's currency.

LESSON DESCRIPTION

Visuals 1-4 explain the demand for and supply of foreign exchange in international currency markets. This is mostly discussion led by the teacher, but there is an optional panel discussion at the end of the lesson.

TIME REQUIRED

Two or three class periods. On the first day, explain the basic determinants of the value of a currency. Assign Activity 1 as a homework reading. On the second day, discuss the various events that lead to changes in the demand for the currency, and (optional) conduct the panel discussion.

MATERIALS

★ One transparency each for Visuals 1, 2, 3, and 4.

★ One copy of Activity 1 for each student.

★ Multiple copies of Visual 2, to facilitate explaining the various procedures.

PROCEDURE

1. Show Visual 1 on the overhead or draw it on the board, but cover the label on the vertical axis. If you are discussing the value of the dollar, the Q axis will be measured in dollars. Ask students what the designation will be on the vertical axis. (Answer: You must value the dollar in terms of an international currency. If you pick, say, the Deutschmark (DM), then the label for the vertical axis will be the price of dollars in DM. This is an important point. It helps students see that an appreciation of the dollar means that Germans are willing to pay more DMs per dollar.)

2. Ask the students to list and explain the primary determinants of the demand for dollars and the supply of dollars in international currency markets. (Answer: From lessons 11, 12, and 14, or from other background work they have done, students should understand that the demand for dollars is determined primarily by exports and capital inflows. The supply of dollars is determined primarily by imports and capital outflows. Display Visual 2, which has the demand and supply curves labeled. With this information students should be able to identify factors that affect exports, capital inflows, imports, and capital outflows, and describe their impact on the value of the dollar in international currency markets.)

3. Ask students to discuss what happens to the value of the dollar when the inflation rate in the United States exceeds the inflation rate in Germany (or whatever country you are using). (Answer: A higher rate of inflation in the United States means that prices for U.S. goods are higher, increasing their cost to Germans. German consumers will buy fewer U.S. goods, thus decreasing their demand for dollars. Furthermore, German goods are now relatively cheaper for U.S. citizens than they were before. [When U.S. goods become more expensive, the opportunity cost of purchasing German goods goes down for U.S. consumers.] U.S. citizens will import more Germans goods, supplying more dollars on the international currency market. The impact of both of these actions is to decrease the value of the dollar in international markets. Show the students the top half of Visual 3 to fix this idea in their minds.)

4. Ask students what happens to the value of the dollar when interest rates in the U.S. rise compared to interest rates in Germany. (Answer: Higher interest rates in the U.S. will lead to a capital inflow. For example, Germans will buy more bonds issued by U.S. companies. As they buy these bonds they must first buy dollars in the international currency market. That increases the demand for dollars. Likewise, U.S. citizens who had been investing abroad will now find it more attractive to purchase bonds issued by U.S. companies, reducing capital outflows from the U.S. and decreasing the supply of dollars to world currency markets. For those reasons, the value of the dollar will rise. Show students the bottom half of Visual 3.)

(Here you might discuss the overall environment for investing in a country and how it affects the value of the currency of that country. For example, if the U.S. appears to be a better place for foreigners to invest, the value of the dollar will rise. Typically, whenever there is political or military instability in other countries the value of the dollar rises as investors want to hold their assets in a safe currency. One of the reasons why the peso declined so dramatically in late 1995 was that a Mexican presidential candidate was assassinated. Ensuing political instability created a flight of assets from Mexico, meaning that more pesos were being sold on the international currency market, and the value of the peso fell.)

5. Now discuss the Australian dollar. Suppose that the summer Olympics in Australia in the year 2000 increase the popularity of Australian goods. What will happen to the value of the Australian dollar? *(Answer: We would expect the value of the Australian dollar to rise. Discuss the idea that any time consumer preferences change, the value of the currency for countries where products are more popular will increase. For example, the value of the yen appreciated and the value of the dollar against the yen declined in international currency markets when U.S. consumers started buying more Japanese cars and fewer U.S. cars.)*

6. Display Visual 4, which shows a price floor for a currency. Ask students whether this currency, when it is supported at this price floor, is undervalued or overvalued compared to the market price. *(Answer: This would be an overvalued currency. That is, the price of 4 DM/dollar is greater than the market price for this currency, which is only 3DM per dollar.)* Ask students what will happen as a result of the price floor. *(Answer: The result will be an excess supply of dollars and a balance of payments deficit. [See lessons 11 and 12 for a discussion of the link between the supply of a currency and a balance of payments deficit.] In general, when a currency experiences a balance of trade deficit, we expect that the value of that currency is going to fall in international markets.)*

7. Suppose a country was part of an international agreement in which it agreed to keep the value of its currency at a certain level. In the example we are using, let's say, the U.S. has agreed to keep the dollar at 4DM to the dollar. Why might the other members of the exchange agreement want the U.S. to keep the value of its currency high? *(Answer: If the value of the dollar fell, U.S. goods would be cheaper in international markets. This would lead to an increase in the demand for U.S. goods and a decrease in the demand for German goods by U.S. citizens. German producers would not be happy to see more U.S. goods sold in Germany and fewer German goods sold in the U.S.)*

8. Ask students what options the U.S. has if it has agreed to keep its currency at the level indicated by the price floor in Visual 4. *(Answer: The U.S. might increase interest rates in order to increase the demand for the dollar from foreign investors. Or it might try to reduce inflation in the U.S. compared to the rate of inflation in Germany, also increasing the demand for the dollar. Or U.S. monetary authorities could buy up the surplus dollars. The first two approaches may be unpopular domestically because, in the short run, they tend to slow economic growth and raise unemployment rates. The last approach is a short-term approach, as described in earlier lessons, because a country can only buy up its own currency as long as it has foreign exchange reserves. Once those reserves run out, it can no longer purchase the excess supply of dollars.)*

9. (Optional) Have students read Activity 1. Then conduct a panel discussion, with students playing each of the characters mentioned in the story:

Alan Greenspan, Chairman of the Board of Governors of the U.S. Federal Reserve

Lowdy Yates of the American Association of Manufacturers

Mary Callahan, Spokesperson for Caterpillar, Inc.

Jo Ellen Westree, Owner of a chain of travel agencies

Have other students ask the participants on the panel about their motives and statements. The discussion may range far afield, but try to direct it to points dealing with international exchange rates. Some of the important points that should be brought out in the discussion are summarized below:

A. **Rising interest rates increase the value of the dollar.** The rise in interest rates will attract foreign capital inflows and reduce the amount of U.S. capital that flows out of the country. Together this will increase the value of the dollar in international markets.

B. **Foreign investors in the U.S. do not like to see the value of the dollar fall.** Foreigners who have invested in the U.S. are holding assets denominated in dollar terms. If the value of the dollar falls, then the value of their assets falls. Students will understand that investors do not like to see the value of their assets decline. This is one of the problems that results from U.S. citizens saving so little, compared to people in many other industrialized nations. Although policy makers like Alan Greenspan may be loath to admit it, they must consider how policies affect foreign investors, because we have come to depend on their capital inflow to augment our savings.

C. **Exporters are typically hurt by a rising value of the dollar.** The representatives for Caterpillar and the American Association of Manufacturers, and for exporters in general, are not happy to see the value of the dollar rise. When the value of the dollar rises it makes it more difficult to sell U.S. products abroad. If foreigners have to pay more to buy a dollar, then they have to spend more of their domestic currency to buy U.S. goods. Thus, we typically observe a decline in exports from the U.S. when there is a rise in the value of the dollar (other things being equal). Firms that export might not oppose the increase in interest rates as much if they thought that U.S. inflation was a problem, but they would probably be disinclined to support higher interest rates if they felt the main purpose was to keep foreign investors happy.)

D. **Importers typically benefit from a rising value of the dollar.** The owner of the travel agencies, contrary to her statement in the article, does stand to benefit from the rise in the value of the dollar. When the dollar appreciates, or strengthens, it costs U.S. citizens less to buy foreign currencies, and thus it costs them less to travel abroad. In general, anyone who benefits more from imports than exports will gain whenever the value of the dollar rises in international markets.

E. **People respond predictably to positive and negative incentives.** If something makes a person better off, he or she is more likely to support it; and if it makes somebody worse off, he or she is more likely to oppose it. Self-interest is a powerful factor in economic decisions and public policy issues.

VISUAL 1
SUPPLY AND DEMAND FOR DOLLARS

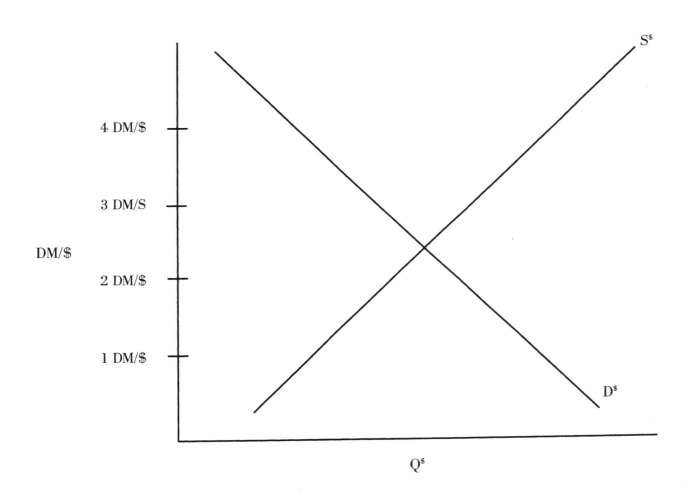

VISUAL 2
SOURCES OF SUPPLY AND DEMAND FOR DOLLARS

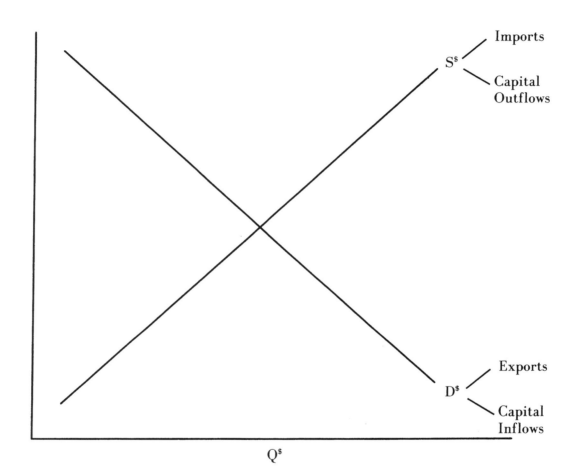

DM/$

S$ Imports

Capital
Outflows

D$ Exports

Capital
Inflows

Q$

VISUAL 3

COMPARING TWO COUNTRIES

The country with the lower inflation rate will experience an increase in the value of its currency that is equal to the difference in the inflation rates between the two countries, other things being equal.

The country with the higher interest rates will experience an appreciation in the value of its currency, other things equal.

VISUAL 4
FIXED EXCHANGE RATE FOR THE DOLLAR

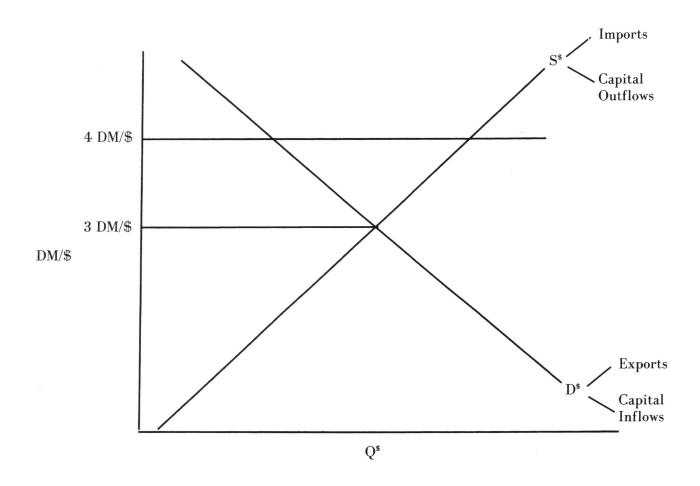

From *Focus: International Economics*, © National Council on Economic Education, New York, NY.

ACTIVITY 1

The following article describes in general terms some events that really have occurred in the U.S. economy, but the article is not a real newspaper article.

Washington (UPX) Alan Greenspan today announced that the Federal Reserve will raise interest rates in the U.S. to fight inflationary pressures in the economy. Critics of Greenspan claim that inflation is not a serious problem, and that the real reason for the rise in interest rates is to prop up the value of the dollar in international markets.

The Caterpillar corporation, which makes large industrial equipment, with nearly 65 percent of its sales coming from overseas markets, complained that the rise in the interest rate would make it more difficult to sell goods abroad. Lowdy Yates, a spokesman for the American Association of Manufacturers, also believes that the increase in interest rates is not needed to fight inflation at this time. According to Yates, "What the Fed is really doing is keeping foreign investors in the United States happy. U.S. citizens have not saved enough in recent years, so we have become dependent on savings from foreigners to finance our investments. The whole purpose of the rise in interest rates is to prop up the value of the dollar to keep foreigners happy."

Caterpillar spokesman Marry Callahan agreed that a rise in U.S. savings rates would let U.S. economic policy decisions be based on what was going on in the U.S. instead of worrying about foreign concerns. But not everyone was offended by the Fed's move. Jo Ellen Westree, owner of a national chain of travel agencies, felt that the Fed's move on interest rates was long overdue. "It is not in my personal interest to see higher interest rates," Westree said, "but I think this is best for the U.S. economy overall."

TRADE WITH JAPAN: HOW FAIR IS IT?

INTRODUCTION

Although there is general agreement that international trade is vitally important in increasing the wealth of nations, there are often disputes about trade. Perhaps the most visible of these disputes has been the one between the U.S. and Japan. Except for Canada, Japan is the United States' most important trading partner. In 1995, U.S. imports from Japan totaled $123.5 billion. However, U.S. exports to Japan that year were only $64.3. The resulting trade deficit of nearly $60 billion, following large deficits in previous years, led to heated debates about whether U.S. trade with Japan is really fair.

This lesson focuses on the U.S. trade relationship with Japan, and more specifically on the free trade vs. fair trade controversy. Students discuss some of the historical reasons why the Japanese economy has been so successful and then analyze some of the key points in the current controversy over U.S.-Japanese trade. Students also learn why the Japanese economy has faltered in recent years.[1]

CONCEPTS

Specialization
Comparative advantage
Balance of trade
Trade deficit
Competition
Trade barriers
Rules of trade

CONTENT STANDARDS

Income for most people is determined by the market value of the productive resources they sell. What workers earn depends, primarily, on the market value of what they produce and how productive they are.

Changes in the structure of the economy, the level of gross domestic product, technology, government policies, and discrimination can influence personal income.

Changes in demand for specific goods and services often affect the incomes of the workers who make those goods and services.

Investment in factories, machinery, new technology, and the health, education, and training of people can raise future standards of living.

Economic growth creates new employment and profit opportunities in some industries, but reduces opportunities in others.

Unemployment imposes costs on individuals and nations. Unexpected inflation imposes costs on many people and benefits some others because it arbitrarily redistributes purchasing power. Inflation can reduce the rate of growth of national living standards, because individuals and organizations use resources to protect themselves against the uncertainty of future prices.

Unemployment can be caused by people changing jobs, by seasonal fluctuations in demand, by changes in the skills needed by employers, or by cyclical fluctuations in the level of national spending.

OBJECTIVES

◆ Identify reasons why Japan has become a world trading power.
◆ Identify and explain sources of controversy related to trade between the U.S. and Japan
◆ Take a position on the free trade vs. fair trade dispute.
◆ Explain recent difficulties in Japan's economy.

TIME REQUIRED

Two class periods.

---

[1]Parts of this lesson are based on *The Japanese Economy: Teaching Strategies*, published by the National Council on Economic Education. Used by permission.

MATERIALS

★ One transparency each for Visuals 1 and 2

★ One copy of Activities 1 and 2 for each student

PROCEDURE

1. Ask students to explain the term "trade deficit." *(Answer: The situation that occurs when the value of a country's imports of goods exceeds the value of its exports of goods.)* Ask why some people object to trade deficits. *(When imports are high, many people in industries that compete with these imports feel their jobs are in jeopardy. This is especially true if people believe that the trade is not fair that is, if there isn't a "level playing field." Persistent trade deficits also indicate that funds borrowed from other nations are being used to pay for the extra imports. Those funds must eventually be repaid.)*

2. Display Visual 1 and discuss the recent U.S. merchandise trade deficits with Japan. Explain that this lesson focuses on why Japan has been successful as an economic power, and explore whether these trade deficits are the result of unfair trade practices. *(Answers to questions on Visual 1: Merchandise trade refers only to goods currently traded, and a deficit means that you purchase more goods than you sell. Other current account items on our balance of payment account [see Lesson 11] with Japan measure trade flows of services, interest earnings, and transfers. Capital account items measure international investment and lending as well as changes in reserves of nations' monetary authorities.)*

3. Have students read Activity 1, Parts 1 and 2. Discuss the questions listed on Visual 2 with the class. Emphasize the difficulties of the Japanese economy in the 1990s and how these difficulties have tarnished the "invincible" image of the Japanese economy. (For more discussion on the Japanese convergence to U.S. income levels over this time period, see Lesson 20 in this volume.)

4. Have two students read (with great expression!) the dialogue between Killigan and Ito from Activity 2. Go over the discussion questions. Have students read their paragraphs (Question 4) to the class. Take a class vote on whether the bill restricting trade with Japan should be passed.

It is important to note that a trade deficit with a particular country is not always an important economic issue. Every country does not have to have a zero deficit with every single trading partner. Also, as Ito points out, a trade deficit must be balanced by a capital account surplus. The U.S. can buy more goods from a country than it sells if that country is willing to invest or lend an equal amount in or to U.S. industries. (Or if other countries are willing to do this.) Overall, Japan's protectionism harms its people more than it harms the U.S. The U.S. standard of living is significantly higher than Japan's. The terms "fair" and "unfair" don't have clear meanings in this discussion.

ASSESSMENT

Have students survey and discuss their parents' views on the issue of restricting Japanese imports. Were parents' views significantly different from those of the students? Discuss why or why not.

U.S. Merchandise Trade Balance with Japan 1991 - 1995 (in millions of dollars)

1991	-43,386
1992	-49,601
1993	-59,355
1994	-65,669
1995	-59,137

Source: *Statistical Abstract of the United States* (from Bureau of Census data)

Questions for Discussion:

1. What is merchandise trade?

2. What does it mean to have a merchandise trade deficit?

3. How does a current account deficit differ from a merchandise trade deficit?

VISUAL 2
DISCUSSION QUESTIONS

1. What were some of the reasons/events that enabled Japan to rise from defeat in WWII and become a world power by the 1970s?

2. Explain how Japan survived the "oil shocks" of the 1970s. Did Japanese companies become stronger or weaker? Why?

3. What characteristics of the Japanese worker have contributed to the success of the Japanese economy?

4. What are some of the difficulties the Japanese economy has recently been experiencing? What is the cause of these difficulties?

ACTIVITY 1, PART 1
JAPAN AS A WORLD POWER: CONTEMPORARY ECONOMIC HISTORY

The immediate post-war period

Japan was occupied by the United States after World War II, from 1945-1951. Under the direction of General Douglas MacArthur, a massive restructuring of Japanese society took place. A new constitution was imposed that gave women the right to vote and recognized labor unions. The occupation also reformed the educational system, carried out land reform, and removed entrenched business leaders, giving younger men an opportunity to rise quickly in the business world. These policies and the revival of trends in Japan that had been blocked by militarism in the 1930s made this occupation one of the most successful in world history. Perhaps the most important factor, however, was the united resolve of the Japanese people to rebuild their nation.

Rapid growth

Aided by huge orders for industrial output brought about by the Korean War and by the gradual opening of the Japanese economy to internal and external competition, the Japanese economy began to grow. By 1951, output had reached 1939 levels. Economic growth continued to increase rapidly from 1955-1971. Although there were minor downturns in some years, the growth rate averaged 10.3 percent per year. (During that time, the much larger American economy averaged 3.4 percent growth annually.) In the 1960s, world trade grew faster than in any previous decade, and Japanese trade grew twice as fast as overall world trade. Japanese products once had the reputation of being inexpensive and shoddy. This perception soon changed as Japanese quality in production came to be recognized in one field after another, including cameras, radios, televisions, tape recorders, cars, steel, and ships. By 1967, exports amounted to 10 percent of Japan's GDP.

One reason the Japanese became so competitive in world trade is that they made large investments in plants and equipment. The cost of borrowing funds for industrial investment was low because of very high personal saving rates. In 1995, Japanese households saved 12.8 percent of their disposable income, versus 3.9 percent in the U.S. Some economists argue that another reason for Japanese competitiveness is that the government's regulatory, monetary, and fiscal policies kept Japanese interest rates and the value of the yen on world currency markets low, which made Japanese products very affordable in world markets.

OPEC in the 1970s

Japan and most other industrialized nations were hit hard by OPEC price increases for oil in 1970s. Japan depended on imports for over 90 percent of its energy consumption, and many observers predicted that the Japanese post-war "miracle" was over. For a year or two inflation increased, but tight monetary policy helped to control that, and Japanese industry developed many new energy-efficient technologies and became even more cost efficient.

Continued progress

Encouraged by tax breaks and other government incentives, Japanese companies were quick to invest in industries of the future, such as electronics, machine tools, computers, and robots. By 1980, Japan had half of the industrial robots in the world. New plant investment led to a 20 percent rise in productivity between 1974 and 1980, and "Made in Japan" became a sign of high quality in consumer products throughout the world.

One of the most important economic changes in the 1980s was the growing interdependence of the American and Japanese economies. Persistent large budget deficits in the U.S. helped to keep U.S. interest rates high, which drew funds from investors in foreign countries like Japan. High U.S. interest rates also increased the value of the dollar in the early 1980s, making American goods more expensive on world markets. These

ACTIVITY 1, PART 1 (continued)

events, combined with relaxed financial regulations in Japan and a rapid fall in real oil prices, led to a large trade surplus for Japan with the U.S. and many other countries year after year.

These persistent trade surpluses created "trade friction" between Japan and the other countries, and trade became a major political and economic issue. In the late 1980s, the Group of Five leading industrial countries implemented policies that lowered the value of the dollar relative to the yen. As the dollar fell, many Japanese companies lost their competitive advantage over U.S. and other Asian exporters. However, even though exports from Japan fell and imports rose, foreign buyers were still willing to pay more for Japanese products which they perceived as better in quality. This and other factors, such as increasing domestic demand in Japan, helped Japanese companies survive and prosper. In fact, in some markets such as VCRs and CD players, American competitors disappeared for a time.

In this period, the Japanese government subsidized declining Japanese industries, thus tying up resources in those industries. Government policies also protected smaller and midsize companies, shielding them from foreign competition. That sowed the seeds for many future problems.

Recent years

In the 1990s the Japanese economy faltered. By 1997, the Nikkei stock average had fallen 50 percent from its 1989 high. From 1992-1995, annual economic growth was only a bit over 1 percent. Although large, highly competitive multinational companies such as Toyota and Sony still prospered, Japanese industries based in the domestic economy such as banks, construction, local manufacturing, and retailing were struggling.

These troubled industries, composed mainly of small and midsize companies, employ about 70 percent of the Japanese workforce. For years they were protected by government policies that shielded them from international competition. Eventually it became harder and harder to protect these industries, as their costs became increasingly higher compared to those of competing firms from other nations.

The Japanese government initiated reforms to force these companies to compete more effectively. However, these reforms were difficult for many Japanese firms and workers to face. Some economists estimate that the actual Japanese unemployment rate is significantly higher than the official 3.5 percent rate (late 1997). To keep employment high, there is currently a great deal of pressure to increase government spending on public projects of dubious long-term value. Many analysts question the wisdom of these policies, and the scale of this problem is substantial. For example, as a percentage of gross national product, Japan's 1995 budget deficit was larger than any of the other leading industrialized nations in the world.

The future

What does the future hold for Japan? Will its economic reforms be successful? Will the "second tier" companies of the Japanese economy become as competitive as the large, highly successful multinational corporations? The Japanese people are highly educated and disciplined, and they have responded well to past economic challenges. As always, only time will tell how well they meet today's problems and what effects their responses will have on the rest of the world's economies.

ACTIVITY 1, Part 2
JAPAN AS A WORLD ECONOMIC POWER: REASONS FOR JAPANESE SUCCESS

Japan was a defeated power in 1945. It was a nation with high population density and few natural resources. As the previous portion of the reading indicates, Japan went on to become one of the world's leading industrial powers. What factors explain this success?

The Japanese worker. The Japanese worker is one of the major causes for the success of the Japanese economy. Japanese workers have a reputation for working very hard. They have a high concern for quality and possess excellent academic skills. They are also very reliable, and are reluctant to show up late or call in sick, because they don't want to let their bosses and co-workers down. Japanese workers are also known for their cooperation and loyalty to their businesses. In part, this reflects Japan's system of lifetime employment. In large Japanese companies, workers expect firms to employ them throughout most of their working lives. Because they do not fear the loss of their jobs, workers are less concerned about the introduction of new labor-saving technologies than workers in the U.S. and other industrialized nations.

A less attractive side of the labor situation is Japan's "dual economy." Only about 30 percent of the workforce enjoys the security of lifetime employment. Many Japanese work in small shops where wages and benefits are low, and job security is dependent on swings in the economy. Furthermore, there are signs that the policy of lifetime employment is weakening in Japan. This is because the pressure of international competition is creating the need to downsize many companies while expanding others and creating new ones.

Education. Japanese workers are well trained. Japanese students score very high on international tests. Japan trains as many engineers each year as we do in the U.S.—a country

with over twice Japan's population. In short, Japan continues to make significant investments in human capital.

Capital investment. The Japanese have made major investments in physical capital, resulting in significant increases in productivity. Major investments in physical capital continue, but recently overinvestments in physical capital have resulted in very low rates of return on investments and low productivity growth.

Role of government. The Japanese government has provided incentives and administrative guidance to the private sector. Although the Japanese economy is basically market-oriented, Japan's government officials, particularly in the Ministry of Trade and Industry (MITI), keep track of international trends and encourage private investment in promising new technologies and markets. MITI has been useful when an industry in Japan winds down, helping firms to merge or make transitions to more promising sectors of the economy. In most cases, there is far less antagonism between government and business in Japan than in the West, and it is assumed that government officials and business people can cooperate.

However, the recent difficulties of the Japanese economy have caused many analysts to believe that the heavy involvement of government agencies like MITI has ultimately been bad for the Japanese economy. This is because the agencies have shielded many smaller domestic companies from the rigors of international competition. These companies are now finding it very difficult to compete in the international and domestic marketplace.

It is also pointed out that MITI did not support Japanese industry's entry into some areas that proved to be Japan's most successful, such

---

ACTIVITY 1, Part 2 (continued)

as automobiles and electronics.

Technological innovation. Japanese firms have been at the cutting edge of many new technologies. Japanese firms still bring many new consumer products to market more quickly and with better quality than American firms. Production engineering and plant design have been key ingredients in Japan's rise to world competition.

It is interesting to note that the Japanese themselves say they owe their success in quality control and productivity to an American college professor, W. Edwards Deming, because of his work in these areas. The Japanese even give an annual award named after Professor Deming to recognize the Japanese company that achieves the greatest gains in quality control

The future. The economic problems that have emerged recently in Japan are forcing the Japanese to reevaluate many of their past economic policies. Many leaders are calling for less government intervention in the economy. They want less regulation of business and less protection of domestic industry from the discipline of international competition. Although Japan's large multinational corporations are still highly competitive, it remains to be seen whether the rest of the Japanese economy can respond to the challenges of the global marketplace.

ACTIVITY 2
U.S. TRADE WITH JAPAN: FREE OR FAIR?

Since 1950 the U.S. and Japan have developed a complex and vital trade relationship. Without a doubt, both nations would be much poorer without each other. However, as with most partnerships, there is a tendency to take things for granted until disagreements arise. In recent years, the most obvious disagreement has been over the balance of trade. The U.S. merchandise trade deficit with Japan averaged over $55 billion from 1991-1995. This means that the U.S. purchased about $55 billion more in goods each year from Japan than Japan purchased from the U.S. This led to calls in the U.S. for protectionist trade measures such as quotas and tariffs. Many in the U.S. believe that "free" trade with Japan is not "fair" trade for U.S. firms and workers. As you will see in the reading below, the issue is not simple. Consider the following dialogue between Yoshi Ito, Japanese trade representative, and Jonathan Killigan, U.S. congressman. (These are fictional characters, but the points they make have been made by real speakers in recent news reports.)

A Friendly Discussion About Trade

KILLIGAN: Hello, Mr. Ito. I am glad you have agreed to meet with me. The constituents in my blue-collar district are up in arms about the recent $60 billion trade deficit with your country. Americans are losing high-paying jobs because people are buying too many Japanese products. My new trade bill, which would raise tariffs and quotas on Japanese goods, is absolutely necessary. We need to "level the playing field" of trade between our two countries. We need "fair trade," not "free trade."

ITO: Mr. Killigan, please! You are making Japan the scapegoat. Overall, America is not losing high-paying jobs because of trade with Japan. Anyway, Japanese trade accounts for only about 37 percent of your overall trade deficit. The U.S. trade problem is not just with Japan. Why pick on us? We are a country with very few natural resources. To survive, we must import raw materials and then produce goods to sell to other countries. A nation that lives on trade has to be able to sell its products freely.

KILLIGAN: I'm sorry, but my first priority is to protect jobs in my district. My constituents come first.

ITO: But tariffs and quotas will harm other Americans even more! It will make high quality Japanese goods, such as CD players, TVs, and cars, much more expensive for American consumers. Is that fair to families just struggling to make ends meet? Remember, Americans aren't forced to buy Japanese products! It is really people who trade, not nations.

KILLIGAN: I don't care. "Buy American" is my motto.

ITO: We don't have many tariffs on our goods. How can you insist that our trade isn't fair?

KILLIGAN: Come, come, Mr. Ito. You do have some very high tariffs, especially on agricultural products. Why, I was in Tokyo last month and it cost a fortune to buy a hamburger! There obviously are very real restrictions on certain high quality American products!

ACTIVITY 2 (continued)

ITO: Well, you may be right there, but I still say that the problem is that many of your companies just can't compete.

KILLIGAN: No wonder! Your large companies only buy parts from their Japanese subsidiaries. You freeze our parts suppliers out. Also, you have so much red tape and bureaucracy that it's impossible to get goods into your country. For example, you require safety and health testing in Japan, even though we have already tested our exports here.

ITO: That may have been true in the past, but we have made it much easier now for Americans to do business in Japan. Our large companies are now buying parts where they can get quality and a good price, regardless of where the parts are made. Often they are now made in America! And don't forget, you Americans also have safety and health restrictions, and they haven't stopped us. We meet the standards, and then some!

KILLIGAN: It's still very difficult for Americans to do business in Japan. Your government needs to do much more to relax customs and rules and to make it easier to do business.

ITO: But my dear Killigan, that is because Americans don't understand our culture! You don't take the time to cultivate business relationships like we do here. You must learn the formal nature of how we do business. Your business people don't even take the time to learn our language. Also, your time horizons are too short. If an American business venture in Japan doesn't show profits quickly, it is dropped. Our companies look at the long term. That's how you improve at trade.

KILLIGAN: It would be foolish for many Americans to learn Japanese. English is now the international trade language. When Japanese people learn English it enables them to communicate in business with many nations, not just one.

ITO: Perhaps. But don't forget, Mr. Killigan, that when Japan runs a current account trade surplus with the U.S., we turn around and invest most of the extra dollars we earn back in the U.S. We build plants here, hiring American workers, or we buy U.S. government securities, helping to finance your budget deficits.

KILLIGAN: Look here, Mr. Ito. If anyone has a budget deficit now it is Japan. In terms of a percentage of GDP, it is higher than any other major nation! If your government would quit subsidizing and protecting your companies, our firms could compete easily. As I said, it's fair trade I'm after: a level playing field!

ITO: I can see that we just don't see eye to eye on this issue. But just remember, passing tariffs and quotas can have disastrous consequences. It can create a chain reaction, like the tariffs in the 1930s, limiting overall world trade and making everyone poorer! Certainly you realize that, don't you?

KILLIGAN: I'm willing to take that chance, as risky as it may be. But perhaps we need to talk about this some more. The vote to impose tariffs on Japanese goods is tomorrow at 5:00 p.m. I'll meet you here tomorrow at noon.

ACTIVITY 2
DISCUSSION QUESTIONS

1. Briefly describe the various ways to limit or hinder trade that were mentioned in the Killigan-Ito exchange.

2. Under each name, list some of the specific arguments for and against the trade bill that were mentioned by Killigan and Ito.

<u>Killigan</u> (for)   <u>Ito</u> (against)

3. What do think Mr. Killigan's strongest argument was? What was Mr. Ito's strongest argument?

4. Write a one- or two-paragraph response to complete and develop one of the following statements. You may be asked to read your response to the class.

   • Although the issue is complex, I believe the current Japan-U.S. trade controversy is more the fault of Japan than the U.S. because...

   • Although the issue is complex, I believe the current Japan-U.S. trade controversy is more the fault of the U.S. than Japan because...

SHOULD A DEVELOPING COUNTRY HAVE FREE TRADE?

INTRODUCTION

Arguments for and against free trade often seem technical and abstract, but there is a strong human dimension underlying these debates. Who are the people who lose jobs to increased foreign competition, and who benefits from lower prices and more efficient production? Are the potential long-term gains worth the short-term costs? This lesson presents pros and cons of removing a protective tariff in a hypothetical Latin American country, from the perspective of people who live there. Students gain insight into the rationale behind these arguments and into some of the problems developing countries face in general.

CONCEPTS

Developing countries
Trade barriers
Tariffs
Imports
Exports

CONTENT STANDARDS

Different methods can be used to allocate goods and services. People, acting individually or collectively through government, must choose which methods to use to allocate different kinds of goods and services.

National economies vary in the extent to which they rely on government directives (central planning) and signals from private markets to allocate scarce goods, services, and productive resources.

Income for most people is determined by the market value of the productive resources they sell. What workers earn depends, primarily, on the market value of what they produce and how productive they are.

Changes in the structure of the economy, the level of gross domestic product, technology, government policies, and discrimination can influence personal income.

Investment in factories, machinery, new technology, and the health, education, and training of people can raise future standards of living.

Economic growth is a sustained rise in a nation's production of goods and services. It results from investments in human and physical capital, research and development, technological change, and improved institutional arrangements and incentives.

OBJECTIVES

◆ Analyze perspectives on the effects of eliminating a protective tariff in a hypothetical developing country.
◆ Rank the relative importance of reasons for eliminating and keeping a protective tariff.
◆ Explain opinions about the value of protective tariffs in developing countries.

LESSON DESCRIPTION

Students play the role of newspaper reporters in a hypothetical Latin American country; they form opinions about a protective tariff in order to write an editorial for a newspaper in the country's capital.

TIME REQUIRED

One class period, with an optional homework assignment.

MATERIALS

★ One copy of Activities 1, 2, and 3 for each student
★ A transparency of Visual 1 (optional)
★ A transparency of a recent editorial from a local newspaper

PROCEDURE

1. Tell the students that today they will take on the role of newspaper reporters in a developing country, writing a story about a controversy: should the country engage in free trade, or should it limit free trade by using protectionist

policies such as tariffs? If students are not familiar with the terms *developing country, Latin America, trade barrier, tariff, comparative advantage, import,* and *export,* display Visual 1 and review the definitions. Point out to students that there is really no clear rule to distinguish between a developing and a developed country. Many countries in Africa, Latin America, and Asia are considered to be developing. These include most of the world's population.

2. Review the idea of a newspaper editorial with students. *(An editorial is an article that serves as the official expression of a newspaper's opinion on an issue. Editorials from major papers often have a great deal of influence on public opinion.)* Display a recent editorial from a local paper to show students an example. Identify its main features.

3. Divide students into groups of six, and give each student a copy of Activity 1 and Activity 2. (These activities may also be used by students individually, if you prefer.) Read the "Background" and "Your Job" sections together.

Tell the students to read the summaries of the interviews together in their groups, perhaps with each student reading one summary out loud. Each group should discuss the interviews and should be certain that everyone in the group understands the reasons behind the opinions expressed. They should fill out the answers to Activity 2 and go over the answers together.

4. Give a copy of Activity 3 to each student. Read over the directions together. You may wish to give students an example of how to respond to the statement. *(For example, one reason for wanting to eliminate the tariff is that it would allow large farmers to buy quality equipment at lower prices. You might suggest that, in your opinion, this is a fairly important reason, and*

you give it three stars.) Give students about 10 minutes to complete Activity 3 individually. When they have finished, call on a few students to read some of their responses. Emphasize that there is not one set of correct answers, nor is there only one correct way to evaluate the number of stars assigned on the handout. The purpose of the activity is to help students evaluate their priorities and sort out their opinions, which should help them write the editorial. For example, some students may see that they have assigned many more stars to reasons on one side of the issue than the other, indicating that they support that side of the argument. Alternatively, other students may believe that one reason for or against the tariff is much more important than all the others, so they will support that side of the argument.

5. Using Activity 3 for background, assign students to write an editorial for the (hypothetical) Latin American newspaper on the issue of the proposed tariff elimination. The editorial should clearly state whether the paper is for or against the proposal to remove the protective tariff, and why. (You may wish to suggest how long it should be. About 400 words may be appropriate.) Owing to time constraints, you may need to make this a homework assignment. Alternatively, the editorial could be done in groups, forcing the group members to come to a consensus on the issue.

ASSESSMENT

Before you collect the editorials, ask students how many wrote in favor of eliminating the protective tariff and how many wrote against it. Ask a few students on each side of the issue to read their editorials. Summarize the points they bring out; review other arguments they have not considered, if necessary.

VISUAL 1
IMPORTANT TERMS

1. ***Developing Country*** (also called "less developed country" or LDC): Countries characterized by low per capita incomes, rapid population growth, lack of industrialization, illiteracy, poverty, and income inequality. The term "developing" implies that the countries are undergoing growth and making changes to improve their conditions.

2. ***Latin America:*** The area in the Western Hemisphere south of the United States. The name comes from the fact that the majority of the people speak Spanish, Portuguese, or French, all of which flowed from the Latin language.

3. ***Trade Barrier:*** A policy reducing or eliminating free trade in a country.

4. ***Tariff:*** A tax on goods imported into a country.

5. ***Comparative Advantage:*** A principle which states that people or nations can gain by specializing in goods that they can produce at the lowest opportunity cost, and by trading for goods that are more expensive for them to produce.

6. ***Import:*** A good or service produced in a foreign country and sold in your country.

7. ***Export:*** A good or service produced in your country and sold in a foreign country.

ACTIVITY 1
SHOULD A DEVELOPING COUNTRY HAVE FREE WORLD TRADE?

Background

You live in a developing country in Latin America. Your country currently has many policies that make it difficult for foreign companies to sell products there, including high tariffs (taxes on imports). For example, if a foreign company wants to sell agricultural machinery in your country, it must pay a 40 percent tariff. This tariff raises the price of the foreign machinery to buyers in your country. Because of this, many local farmers and ranchers buy the less expensive machinery produced in your country instead of buying the imported machinery, even though the imports are generally acknowledged to be of much higher quality.

A new economic proposal is being debated in your national legislature. This proposal, if it passes, would eliminate this 40 percent tariff on agricultural machinery. This would probably lead to future polices that would reduce or eliminate other trade barriers, opening the doors to free trade in your country.

Your job

You are a reporter for the leading newspaper in the capital city of your country. You are assigned to decide whether your paper should be for or against removing the 40 percent tariff on agricultural machinery. You conducted six interviews with interested citizens and government officials about the proposal to eliminate the tariff.

You must now analyze the information from the interviews and form an opinion for your newspaper about this proposal. Later you will write an editorial for your paper, stating and explaining your newspaper's position on this proposal. Read the summaries of the interviews below. Use this information to complete Activities 2 and 3.

Interview 1: Mr. Juarez

Mr. Juarez's family has been one of the major landholders in your country for over 150 years. He currently owns over 15,000 acres in the northwest region, where he raises cattle and grows wheat, oranges, and vegetables. Mr. Juarez employs over 400 local families as well as professional managers and specialists in agriculture and ranching technology. He recently set up processing facilities to produce orange juice and frozen meat and vegetables, and he maintains offices in the capital city to run his business. He would like to export his foods to other countries.

Mr. Juarez is a strong proponent of free trade. He believes that eliminating the 40 percent tariff on agricultural machinery is a very good idea. In his words, "My country's comparative advantage is in producing agricultural products, because it is relatively inexpensive for us to produce them. On the other hand, it is very expensive for us to produce high-quality agricultural machinery. We should eliminate the tariff, import machinery, and export agricultural products. We will benefit from the increased exports and from lower-priced imports." Mr. Juarez also sees the possibility that a tariff reduction would allow him (and others like him) to expand the amount of land under cultivation and hire more workers. He could then pay higher wages to his workers, because their productivity would increase with their use of the advanced machinery. Since the new machinery would lower the cost of food production, food prices could decrease, benefitting all consumers.

ACTIVITY 1 (continued)

He also points out that other countries have tariffs on the food products grown in your country. If you eliminate your tariffs, other countries will be more likely to eliminate theirs. This would expand the markets for products produced in your country, leading to economic growth and more jobs in the future.

Interview 2: Mr. and Mrs. Baez

To conduct this interview, you travel 150 miles from your capital city along steadily deteriorating roads to a small village named after your country's revolutionary hero. There you find Mr. and Mrs. Baez, who have agreed to be interviewed at their small home. Several small children try to hide behind their parents. Baez family members have farmed in this region for over 80 years, first as tenant farmers and later with their own land. Mr. and Mrs. Baez own 10 acres of land, and they rent another 20 acres from families whose children have moved to the capital city in search of jobs and a better life. The Baez family grows fruit and corn, which they sell to independent truckers. The truckers then sell the food in open-air markets in the larger cities.

Mr. and Mrs. Baez make it very clear that they strongly oppose the tariff reduction proposed for agricultural machinery. Puzzled, you point out that the reduction in tariffs should make the machinery cheaper for them to buy. Mr. Baez agrees with your thinking, but says that he would never be able to use the imported equipment. The new equipment, such as large tractors, is designed for use on large farms. If it becomes available at a lower price it will raise the profits of large farms, enabling them to buy more land like the land that the Baez's now rent. With the present technology, the Baez's can compete effectively with the large farmers, given their need for hired labor and absentee management. However, this would not be the case if tariffs were eliminated. Mrs. Baez emotionally calls out the name of your country's revolutionary leader and declares that small farmers will not be pushed off their land.

Interview 3: Mr. Rodriguez

Mr. Rodriguez is the manager of a manufacturing firm near the capital city, which produces agricultural machinery. Some of the machinery he produces is similar to the machinery being considered for the tariff reduction. He is, not surprisingly, very much opposed to eliminating the tariff. If his business loses sales to imports, local workers would lose their jobs. He points out that he employs over 800 people as skilled production workers who earn wages above those earned by non-manufacturing employees.

Mr. Rodriguez goes on to say that the timing of the tariff proposal couldn't be worse. Over the last three months, he has been negotiating with a Japanese firm for the rights to manufacture their line of farm equipment in your country. If the negotiations for this partnership are successful, the Japanese firm will finance the construction of additional plants and provide supervisors to ensure that the plants are operating efficiently.

In two to three years, Mr. Rodriguez predicts that they will be able to produce high quality farm equipment for export to the rest of the world. They would be able to use the Japanese company's distribution and marketing network for this purpose. At the end of five years, it may be possible to employ up to 5,000 workers in your country, if the Japanese company can be brought in "It is essential," says Mr. Rodriguez, "that the tariff barriers remain for the next five years if the agreement with the Japanese is to be signed. The start-up costs and training expenses associated with a new plant are too expensive to undertake without the assurance of having a protected internal market to sell to during this initial stage of operation."

ACTIVITY 1 (continued)

Interview 4: Ms. Sanchez

Ms. Sanchez is a government official representing the Finance Ministry in your country. When you mention the proposed tariff reduction, she launches into a strong statement in favor of the proposal. She is an advocate of free trade, both in principle and practice. She says that only through free trade can a country become a strong and efficient competitor in world markets. Ms. Sanchez envisions a time in the not-so-distant future when your country has higher living standards with vastly improved systems of health care and education. She believes that economic growth is necessary to achieve these goals. For this to occur, your industries must be able to compete with foreign industries. Protective tariffs on inefficient industries slow down this growth potential, and result in increased prices to consumers as well.

"Our country needs to export more to strengthen our trade position," she states. "If we relax our trade barriers and are more open to imports, other countries will be more likely to buy our exports. This means jobs for our people in industries where we can be competitive."

Additionally, Ms. Sanchez points out that the International Monetary Fund and the international banking community are very concerned about the amount of money the government and businesses in your country owe to foreign banks. Many foreign companies are reluctant to invest in your country because they perceive a lack of freedom for businesses. Ms. Sanchez believes that a combination of reduced trade barriers and increased export sales would increase international confidence in your economy and help attract foreign capital necessary for economic growth.

Interview 5: Mr. Lopez

Mr. Lopez is a government official representing the Ministry of Land and Industry in your country. When you mention the proposed tariff reduction, he attacks the idea for several reasons. He states that he has been working for years to expand your country's manufacturing base. He believes that only through increased manufacturing jobs can the vast pool of labor in your country be employed at a livable wage. He says that protecting the relatively new manufacturing industries in your country from foreign competition is the only way to make this work. Once your country has developed its manufacturing base, aided by protective tariffs, it may be in a position to increase exports.

Mr. Lopez also says that he opposes removing the tariff because he wants to preserve and protect the tropical rainforest in your country. "Opening up trade will encourage profit-seeking people to produce goods to export to other countries. Our country already successfully exports minerals, timber, and agricultural products on a smaller scale. People may have incentives to buy inexpensive rainforest land and clear it to produce these products. But the problem is that once deforestation has taken place, the rainforest is rarely able to regenerate itself. We risk forcing many species of plants and animals into extinction that grow only there. Profits for people today may result in irreparable harm to future generations."

Interview 6: Mrs. Miranda

Mrs. Miranda lives in a small house in the poorest section of the capital city. She has three small children. She does sewing work for as many hours as she can each day, producing soccer balls at home; she sells the soccer balls to a sporting goods company. These balls are eventually sold in the United States. She supports the policy that would end the tariffs for two reasons: "The most important thing to me is food for my children and my job, even though I can only work part time. Better farming in this country would mean lower food prices for my children. My job might be lost if other countries put tariffs on the things I make. I didn't understand this until I found a job making things that people from other countries buy, but now I do."

ACTIVITY 2
ARGUMENTS FOR AND AGAINST FREE TRADE IN A DEVELOPING COUNTRY

DIRECTIONS:

For each of the six interviews, make a check mark to indicate whether the person was in favor of the protective tariff or opposed to it. Then summarize the reasons each offered to support his or her position.

1. Mr. Juarez: _____Eliminate the tariff   _____Keep the tariff
   Why?

2. Mr. and Mrs. Baez: _____Eliminate the tariff   _____Keep the tariff
   Why?

3. Mr. Rodriguez: _____Eliminate the tariff   _____Keep the tariff
   Why?

4. Ms. Sanchez: _____Eliminate the tariff   _____Keep the tariff
   Why?

5. Mr. Lopez: _____Eliminate the tariff   _____Keep the tariff
   Why?

6. Ms. Miranda: _____Eliminate the tariff   _____Keep the tariff
   Why?

ACTIVITY 2, ANSWERS
ARGUMENTS FOR AND AGAINST
FREE TRADE IN A DEVELOPING COUNTRY

1. Mr. Juarez: _____✔_____ Eliminate the tariff _____ Keep the tariff

Why? *Mr. Juarez is a major landholder who farms, ranches, and processes food products. He wishes to export his products and believes that eliminating the tariffs may open up foreign markets. He believes in countries specializing according to their comparative advantage and trading with others, and he maintains that his country has the comparative advantage in producing food, not machinery. He thinks that importing machinery at lower prices would allow his businesses to expand and become more productive. He could therefore hire more workers and pay higher wages. Food prices could also go down, both at home and abroad.*

2. Mr. and Mrs. Baez :_____ Eliminate the tariff _____✔_____ Keep the tariff

Why? *As small farmers, Mr. and Mrs. Baez feel that the imported machinery will not help them and, in fact, will help large farmers at their expense. The imported machinery can be more efficiently used on large farms, and it will raise large farmers' profits and encourage them to expand. This may make it difficult for small farmers to continue to rent land and compete with the large farms. Keeping the tariff would maintain higher prices of the imported machinery, lowering the profits of the potentially more efficient large farms. This is the only way that small farmers could stay in business, and Mr. and Mrs. Baez do not want to move off their land.*

3. Mr. Rodriguez: _____ Eliminate the tariff _____✔_____ Keep the tariff

Why? *Mr. Rodriguez wants to keep the tariff to protect his agricultural machinery business from foreign competition. If he went out of business, his workers would be unemployed. He believes that in the future his business will be able to compete more effectively with imports because he hopes to establish an agreement with a Japanese firm to manufacture their line of farm equipment. If all goes well, he believes that in five years he, with Japanese assistance, will be a large and efficient manufacturer of farm equipment, able to compete in international markets. He says it is possible then that he would be open to removing the tariff then.*

4. Ms. Sanchez: _____✔_____ Eliminate the tariff _____ Keep the tariff

Why? *Ms. Sanchez believes that free trade would enable the country to progress and become competitive in world markets. The country would be able to raise its standard of living and improve health care and education. She wants to increase exports to create jobs, and she believes that relaxing trade barriers will help achieve this goal. The country is experiencing difficulty in borrowing from abroad because of current high debts, and foreign investment is not as high as it could be. Ms. Sanchez believes that eliminating trade barriers would show that the country is trying to solve its problems and may instill international confidence in the country, leading to economic growth.*

ACTIVITY 2, ANSWERS (continued)

5. Mr. Lopez: _____ Eliminate the tariff ___✔___ Keep the tariff

Why? *Mr. Lopez believes that the tariff is necessary to protect the new manufacturing industries* in the country, and that manufacturing jobs are necessary to provide employment at decent wages. Once the manufacturing sector is established, they may be able to export and compete with foreign companies. He also believes that opening up trade may lead to destruction of the fragile rainforest, because people seeking profits in export markets will have incentives to cut down the trees and convert the forest into agricultural or mining lands.

6. Mrs. Miranda: ___✔___ Eliminate the tariff _____ Keep the tariff

Why? Mrs. Miranda wants lower food prices so that it will be easier to feed her children, and she does not want to risk losing her job if other countries impose tariffs on the soccer balls she helps to produce in her part-time job.

ACTIVITY 3
PRIORITIZE YOUR OPINIONS: SHOULD A DEVELOPING COUNTRY HAVE FREE TRADE?

You have read and summarized six interviews about whether a developing country should eliminate a protective tariff and move toward free trade. You may have found that there are important arguments on both sides of the question, and that sometimes the interviews provide conflicting information. For example, people for and against the protective tariff believe that more jobs will be created for people in the developing country if their opinion is followed. To complete your assignment for the newspaper, you must decide if you are for or against removing the tariff.

Look through your notes on Activity 2 for the people who were in favor of the proposal to eliminate the tariff (in favor of freer trade). List the five reasons that you think were most convincing to support this opinion. After each reason, indicate how important you think that reason is by assigning one-to-five stars. (One star means that you think the reason is of minor importance; five means that you think the reason is crucially important.) Do the same for the people who were against the proposal to eliminate the tariff (against freer trade). Then write your conclusion in the space provided.

Five Important Reasons to Eliminate the Protective Tariff	How strongly I Feel About This Reason (*/ **/ ***/ ****/ *****)
1.	
2.	
3.	
4.	
5.	

CONCLUSION:
MY NEWSPAPER SHOULD BE (FOR/AGAINST) _____ THE PROPOSAL TO ELIMINATE THE PROTECTIVE TARIFF ON AGRICULTURAL MACHINERY.

THE NAFTA DEBATE

INTRODUCTION

The U.S. Congress passed the North American Free Trade Agreement (NAFTA) in 1994. The debate surrounding the agreement was hotly contested. In the United States, conservative and liberal politicians, as well as labor unions, environmentalists, and representatives of big business, continue to take sides on this issue. Some fear that freer trade will cause a great loss of jobs, while others expect consumers to benefit from lower prices on Mexican and Canadian goods. Internationally, concern has arisen among countries not included in the NAFTA agreement, especially those in South and Central American. There is a fear that they will not be able to compete with the Canadian, American and Mexican goods that are now relatively less expensive and easier to move and sell across Canada, the United States, and Mexico. While the specific examples in this lesson apply only to the United States and Mexico, the issues and concepts apply in all free trade areas.

CONCEPTS

Free trade agreements
Tariffs
Trade policy

CONTENT STANDARDS

Income for most people is determined by the market value of the productive resources they sell. What workers earn depends, primarily, on the market value of what they produce and how productive they are.

Changes in demand for specific goods and services often affect the incomes of the workers who make those goods and services.

Investment in factories, machinery, new technology, and the health, education, and training of people can raise future standards of living.

Economic growth creates new employment and profit opportunities in some industries, but growth reduces opportunities in others.

OBJECTIVES

◆ Illustrate the effects of imposing or eliminating tariffs, using a supply and demand model.
◆ Identify the major groups who gained and lost as a result of NAFTA.

LESSON DESCRIPTION

In this lesson, students use supply and demand curves to study the effects of tariffs. They start with an equilibrium situation and work through the price and quantity effects of a tariff. They also learn to identify who gained and who lost when the North American Free Trade Agreement was implemented.

TIME REQUIRED

Three to four class periods. Day one: start Activity 1 . Day two: finish Activity 1 and begin Activities 2 and 3. Day three: finish Activities 2 and 3.

MATERIALS

★ One copy of Activities 1, 2, 3, and 4 for each student.
★ A transparency of Visual 1

PROCEDURE

1. Distribute a copy of Activity 1 to each student and instruct students to read Parts I and II. To make sure students understand the chart, ask the following questions:

   A. What is the quantity demanded when the price is $8 a yard? *(5,000,000 yards)*

   B. What is the price producers would require to produce and sell 5,000,000 yards? *($8.00)*

2. Have the students complete Figure 1 and answer the following questions:

   A. What is the equilibrium price and quantity? *(Price = $8 per yard and Quantity = 5 million yards)*

B. Does the amount the consumer pays exactly equal the amount the producer receives and keeps? *(Yes. All the money that the consumer pays goes to the producer.)*

C. If the price rises to $10 per yard, how much would be demanded? *(4,000,000 yards)*

3. Have the students read Part III of Activity 1 and discuss the following questions:

A. Ask students for a common example where the price the producer receives is different from the price the buyer pays. *(State or local sales taxes are perhaps the easiest examples to use. When a consumer buys a music CD, the price may be $12. However, when she pays for that CD, she will pay $12 plus the sales tax. The record store keeps only $12; the tax is paid by the store to the government.)*

B. If the sales tax is 5%, how much does the buyer pay for a music CD that costs $12? *($12 times the tax rate. If the sales tax is 5%, then she would pay $.60 in tax and the market price would be $12.60.)*

C. What happens to the $.60 tax the consumer pays? *(The seller does not get to keep it. The store owner must give it to the government.)*

D. What happens to the rest of the money? *(The seller keeps this to pay for labor and other costs, and to realize a profit on the sale. The producer price is $12.)*

4. Have the students read Part IV of Activity 1 and complete Tables 2 and 3. *You will notice in the suggested answers for Table 2, Activity 1, that at a given quantity the producer price plus the tariff is equal to the producer price plus $6. For example, at a quantity of 3.5 million, the producer price plus tariff is equal to $2 + $6 = $8. At a quantity of 5 million, the producer price plus the tariff is equal to $8 + $6 = $14.*

In Table 3 the column for demand remains unchanged from Table 1. However, the column for supply coincides with the results from Table 2.

5. Have the students draw the demand curve, the supply curve, and the new supply (including tariff) on Figure 2. Ask and discuss the following questions:

A. Has the U.S. demand for Mexican textiles changed? *(No. The consumers' decision is based on market price. The price increases resulting from the tariff reduce the quantity demanded, but do not change the demand curve or schedule.)*

B. Has the Mexican supply of textiles to the U.S. changed? Another way of asking this question is, what is the difference between the two supply curves? *(At every quantity, the producer now requires the market price to be $6 higher than before to supply the same amount. In effect, the tariff represents an additional cost that producers must cover for each unit they sell.)*

C. After the tariff, at what market price is quantity demanded equal to quantity supplied? *(Price = $10 per yard and Quantity = 4 million yards.)*

D. What effect did the tariff have in this market? *(The market price has risen $2 and the quantity has fallen by 1 million.)*

E. What happened to the producer price? *(Notice that the producer does not gain from the increased price. Although the price rose $2, there was a $6 tax. This means the price producers received really fell $4. The seller's revenues fell from $40 million [$8 x 5,000,000] to $16 million [$4 x 4,000,000].)*

6. Ask the following questions to the class before showing Visual 1:

A. What is the economic relationship between U.S. textiles and Mexican textiles? *(They are substitutes goods; Mexican textile producers compete with U.S. textile producers.)*

B. What effect does the increase in the market price for Mexican textiles coming to the U.S. have on the demand for American textiles in the U.S? *(When the price of a Mexican textile increases the demand for the other U.S. textiles will increase.)*

7. Display Visual 1. Mention that the new demand curve represents the increase in demand for U.S. textiles resulting from the increase in the price of Mexican textiles.

A. What happens to equilibrium price and quantity for U.S. textiles? (They both rise.)

B. What happened to total revenue in the American textile market? *(Because both price and quantity increase, total revenue has to rise. Specifically, revenue increases from $30 million [$3 x 10 million] to $44 million [$4 x 11 million].)*

C. Explain to the class that nothing discussed so far has changed income levels in the U.S. If U.S. income stays the same, but more money is being spent on American textiles, what does that say must be happening in some other market? *(First, you should point out that, after the tariff, U.S. citizens are spending the same amount on Mexican textiles. If more is spent on American textiles, then there must be some market in the economy [and we may have trouble identifying it] where demand must fall. If more of our budget is going into one market, then some other market must suffer.)*

Note that if we were to work this example in reverse, lifting the tariff, then the American textiles market would suffer. In that case, since we are removing a tariff on Mexican textiles, we will be able to identify which market is hurt (American textiles).

8. Distribute a copy of Activities 2 and 3 to each student and tell the students to read the instructions at the top of Activity 2. Explain that there is a big debate over the merits of NAFTA. Remind students that imposing a tariff hurts some sectors of the economy, so protection is not necessarily a good thing. It helped the U.S. textile industry in our example, but it must have hurt some other U.S. industry. Given this outcome, it is not surprising that there is a debate about whether or not removing tariffs is a good thing. Some parties will be hurt and some will be helped. These activities will help students identify the arguments for and against NAFTA.

9. Instruct students to complete Activity 2. As an extension activity for high-ability classes, send students to the library to find articles presenting additional arguments for or against NAFTA. A further extension could be to ask students to write a paper arguing for one side or the other in the debate.

10. Reproduce the empty table from Activity 2 on the board or project it as a visual. Have the class help fill in the table by listing the arguments for and against NAFTA that they found in the article from Activity 3. When the table has been completely filled in, ask the students whether they think there is a clear right or wrong answer when it comes to supporting or opposing NAFTA. Explain to students that although it is difficult to get an accurate overall measure of the costs and benefits of NAFTA, it is widely accepted among U.S. economists that NAFTA and free trade have net benefits for the economy as a whole.

ASSESSMENT

1. Distribute Activity 4 to the class. Instruct students to work individually to decide which groups listed would be for, against, or undecided about NAFTA. Encourage them to identify any other groups that would support or oppose NAFTA.

2. Have individuals report their answers. Suggested answers:

A. *U.S. Trade unions: Some trade unions would be against NAFTA on the grounds that it will displace many U.S. workers by making it easier for their jobs to move to Mexico, where workers will receive less pay and work under harder or less safe conditions. However, unions that represent workers with jobs in export industries may well favor NAFTA, hoping to gain more jobs and higher wages.*

B. *Mexican consumers: Mexican consumers would be for NAFTA because it will increase the variety and quality of the goods available to them and it will lower their prices.*

C. *Environmentalists: One could make an argument that environmentalists would be for NAFTA because, by making the Mexican people wealthy, it may lead them to demand a better environment. One could also say that the trade agreement does not enable easy enforcement of environmental standards; and, with more production in Mexico, pollution of the water and air will increase, given weaker government standards on the environment in Mexico. In general, environmental groups have opposed NAFTA.*

D. *Asian textile manufacturers: Asian textile manufacturers will most likely be against NAFTA for two reasons. First, it will make Mexican and Canadian textiles relatively cheaper in the U.S. when tariffs are lifted on textiles from those countries but maintained on Asian textiles. Second, the agreement has encouraged partnerships between the U.S. and Mexican producers of textiles, allowing those firms to compete more effectively with other world textile producers.*

E. *The American and Mexican textile and clothing business: NAFTA reduces the protection these businesses received against imports from the partner country. If these businesses wanted to continue to receive protection, they would oppose NAFTA. However, they might seek a different advantage. NAFTA has encouraged partnerships between the textile industries in the two countries. The agreement has helped them compete against firms from other countries, so they might support it.*

F. *The country of Chile: Chile could be harmed as an outsider country (see item D, above), so Chile might oppose NAFTA. But Chile might see a great potential advantage arising from NAFTA. There has been talk of including Chile in the next round of talks concerning the NAFTA agreement. NAFTA membership would help Chile's trade position immensely. Thus Chile might support NAFTA.*

VISUAL 1
FREE TRADE VERSUS TRADE WITH A TARIFF

Demand for American Textiles in the U.S. and Supply of American Textiles in the U.S.

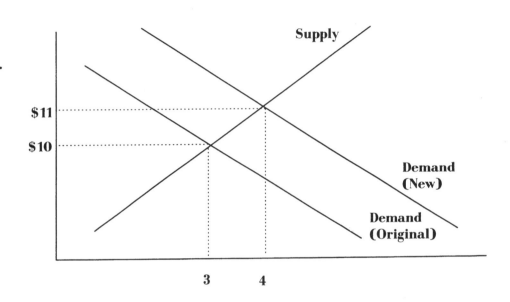

Price for American textiles in the U.S.

Supply

$11

$10

Demand (New)

Demand (Original)

3   4

Quantity of American Textiles in millions

ACTIVITY 1
FREE TRADE VERSUS TRADE WITH A TARIFF

Part I: Overview

To understand the effects of NAFTA, an agreement by which tariffs are being eliminated among Canada, the U.S., and Mexico, supply and demand models can be used to compare and predict outcomes when there is free trade and when there are tariffs. **Free trade** between two countries means there are no tariffs on either country's imports. Tariffs are a kind of barrier to trade. Quotas and other nontariff barriers are also discussed in this activity.

There are actually two types of tariffs. The first type, a **per unit tariff**, occurs when a fixed tax is charged on each unit of a good imported into a country. For an **ad valorem tariff**, the amount taxed is a percentage of the price of the imported good. For example, a \$1 per unit tariff on a good which costs \$20 per unit makes the market price \$21. A 10 percent ad valorem taraiff on a good which costs \$20 makes the price of that good \$20 + \$2 = \$22. In this activity, our examples will use only per unit tariffs. The general direction of effects for this kind of tariff is identical to the direction of effects for an ad valorem tariff, although the size of the effects can be somewhat different.

Part II: Free Trade

Table 1 shows a demand and supply relationship for Mexican textiles sold in the U.S. and the supply of the Mexican textiles sold in the U.S. Price is measured per yard, and quantities are measured in yards of cloth.

Table 1: Supply and Demand for Mexican Textiles

Price for Mexican Textiles (per yard)	Quantity of Mexican Textiles Demanded (Yards)	Quantity of Mexican Textiles Supplied (Yards)
\$2	8,000,000	3,500,000
\$4	7,000,000	4,000,000
\$6	6,000,000	4,500,000
\$8	5,000,000	5,000,000
\$10	4,000,000	5,500,000
\$12	3,000,000	6,000,000
\$14	2,000,000	6,500,000
\$16	1,000,000	7,000,000
\$18	0	7,500,000

ACTIVITY 1 (continued)

Using the information in Table 1, draw a graph of the U.S. Demand for Mexican Textiles and the Supply of Mexican Textiles to the U.S. on the axes below.

Figure 1: Demand for Mexican Textiles in U.S. and Supply of Mexican Textiles to U.S.

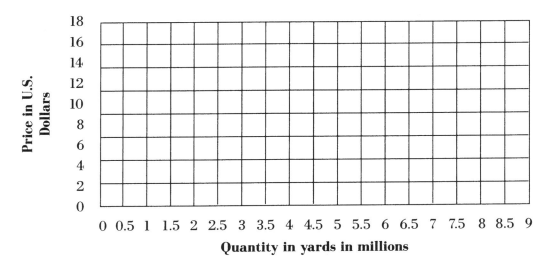

Part III: Understanding Market and Producer Prices

In this section, the effect of a U.S. tariff on Mexican textiles will be analyzed. When a tariff is placed on a good, the price that consumers pay in the market, the **market price**, is different from the price that producers receive. The tariff is built into the price the producer receives for the good, but it must be paid to the government. The amount the producer receives after paying the tariff is called the producer price. The market price now includes the tariff and the producer price. Producers still base the quantity they supply on the price they receive, the producer price. Consumers still base the quantity they demand on the price they pay, the market price.

Part IV: Trade with Tariffs

In Table 1, when there was no tariff, the market price and the producer price were the same. The quantity supplied was determined by the producer price. In Table 2, you are asked to assume a $6 per unit tariff and then to calculate the new price schedule required to maintain the quantities shown. Do this by adding the $6 tariff to the producer price for each quantity.

ACTIVITY 1 (continued)

Table 2: Trade with a $6 per yard tariff

Producer Price for Mexican Textiles	Producer Price plus $6 tariff on Mexican Textiles	Quantity of Mexican Textiles Supplied
$2		3,500,000
$4		4,000,000
$6		4,500,000
$8		5,000,000
$10		5,500,000
$12		6,000,000
$14		6,500,000
$16		7,000,000
$18		7,500,000

In Table 3, fill in the quantity demanded and quantity supplied, given the market price.

Table 3: Supply and Demand for Mexican Textiles

Price for Mexican Textiles *(per yard)*	Quantity of Mexican Textiles Demanded *(Yards)*	Quantity of Mexican Textiles Supplied *(Yards)*
$2		
$4		
$6		
$8		
$10		
$12		
$14		
$16		
$18		

Draw the original supply curve (using data from Table 1) on Figure 2, below. Next draw the supply curve with the tariff (using the data from Table 2). Finally, draw the relationship between market price and quantity demanded.

ACTIVITY 1 (continued)

Figure 2: Demand for Mexican Textiles in U.S. and Supply of Mexican Textiles to the U.S. at the Market Price.

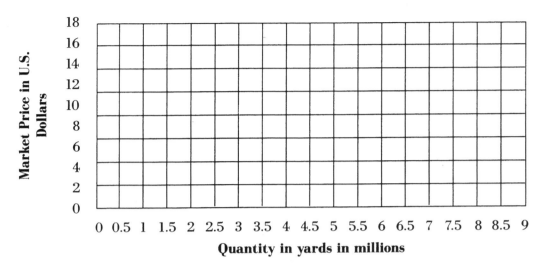

QUESTIONS FOR DISCUSSION:

1. Has the U.S. demand for Mexican textiles changed?

2. At market price, has the Mexican supply of textiles to the U.S. changed?

3. What do you notice about the effects of a tariff?

4. What happened to the producer price?

ACTIVITY 1
ANSWERS (continued)

Below are the answers for the tables and figures that correspond with Activity 1.

Figure 1: Demand for Mexican Textiles in U.S. and Supply of Mexican Textiles to the U.S.

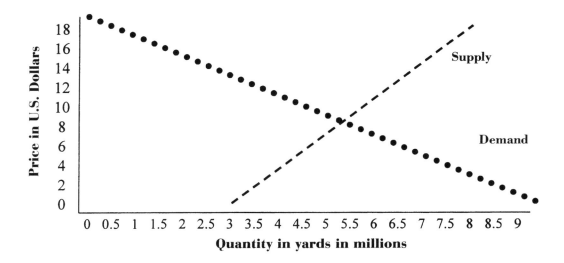

ACTIVITY 1
ANSWERS (continued)

Table 2: Trade with a $6 per yard tariff

Producer Price for Mexican Textiles	Producer Price plus $6 Tariff on Mexican Textiles	Quantity of Mexican Textiles Supplied
$2	$8	3,500,000
$4	$10	4,000,000
$6	$12	4,500,000
$8	$14	5,000,000
$10	$16	5,500,000
$12	$18	6,000,000
$14	$20	6,500,000
$16	$22	7,000,000
$18	$24	7,500,000

Table 3:

Market Price for Mexican Textiles	Quantity of Mexican Textiles Demanded	Quantity of Mexican Textiles Supplied
$2	8,000,000	Not enough information given
$4	7,000,000	Not enough information given
$6	6,000,000	Not enough information given
$8	5,000,000	3,500,000
$10	4,000,000	4,000,000
$12	3,000,000	4,500,000
$14	2,000,000	5,000,000
$16	1,000,000	5,500,000
$18	0	6,000,000

ACTIVITY 1
ANSWERS (continued)

**Figure 2: Demand for Mexican Textiles in the U.S.
and Supply of Mexican Textiles to the U.S.**

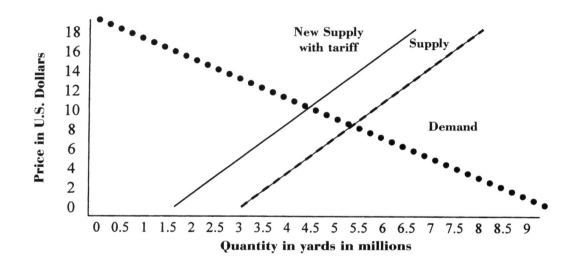

ACTIVITY 2
NAFTA: FOR OR AGAINST

Use information from a copy of Activity 3, **The NAFTA Effect**, from *The Economist*, July 5, 1997, to fill in the chart below.

Arguments for NAFTA	Arguments against NAFTA

ACTIVITY 2, (continued)

Arguments for NAFTA	Arguments against NAFTA

ACTIVITY 2
NAFTA: FOR OR AGAINST
SUGGESTED ANSWERS

Arguments for NAFTA	Arguments against NAFTA
NAFTA has helped Mexican consumers by increasing the variety and quality of goods available to them and by lowering prices.	NAFTA has widened the U.S. trade deficit with Mexico, damaging the U.S. economy.
As the Mexican people become richer, the growing middle class will insist on better working conditions and a healthier environment.	Mexican workers will be exploited by U.S. companies by being paid low wages and by being forced to work in bad conditions.
The losses to U.S. workers are actually not terribly big. Only 117,000 Americans have needed to take the benefits the government offered to those displaced by NAFTA.	American workers will lose jobs to Mexican workers who are willing to take lower pay and work in unhealthy and unsafe conditions.
Even though the economic effect may not be as great as suspected, it has had the effect of putting and keeping Mexico on a path to political and economic reform.	NAFTA will not have as great an economic effect as promised. The U.S. already had low tariffs on most Mexican goods, and Mexico was already freeing up trade after joining GATT (the general agreement on tariffs and trade).
The great changes in Mexico have encouraged other countries like Chile to push for freer trade and increased political reform so that they can join in a trade agreement with the U.S.	NAFTA discriminates against trade from other countries in Asia, the Caribbean, and Central America.
NAFTA, by making the people of Mexico richer, will decrease the number of illegal immigrants into the U.S.	Joining with Mexico means that the U.S. economy is much more dependent on its very unstable neighbor's welfare. This leads to more financial aid and political responsibility toward Mexico.
Increasing the wealth of the Mexican people will mean that fewer of them will turn to drug smuggling for their income.	U.S. firms will invest more in Mexico but will not hold their plants there to the same environmental standards the plants in the U.S. must meet. This will cause water and air pollution in Mexico.

ACTIVITY 3
THE NAFTA EFFECT*

So far, North America's free-trade deal has helped Mexico's economy without hurting the United States. But its chief effect reaches beyond economics.

To some, it was the road to hell: "Free trade equals slave trade," declared one banner in Texas in 1993. According to its enemies, the North American Free-Trade Agreement would suck jobs and investment out of the United States and Canada into their poor southern partner, Mexico. Not that this would do Mexicans any good: it would put them at the mercy of rapacious capitalists pouring filth into Mexico's air and rivers.

To others, especially the governments of the three countries, NAFTA was a distributor of milk and honey. America and Canada, already linked by their own trade deal since 1989, would be enriched by the opening of Mexico's economy; Mexico would rise on a flood of trade with and investment from its wealthy new friends.

Three and a half years later, the quarrels still rage, even if nobody now talks seriously of dropping NAFTA. Politicians in America and Mexico, the countries in which it has been most controversial, continue to debate it fiercely. Next week the Clinton administration is expected to deliver a doubtless glowing report to Congress on NAFTA's economic effects, and will receive an equally predictable raspberry from trade unions and environmentalists. In Mexico, left-wing candidates in the elections due on July 6th would like the treaty revised to allow freer migration of Mexican workers northwards a suggestion that brings raspberries from the northerners. So which side was right: the Jeremiahs or the Panglosses? Neither, by a long chalk. In an economy as large as America's, the effect of freer trade with Mexico was never likely to be great; and so it has proved, Mr. Clinton's report

notwithstanding. In far smaller Mexico, whose economy is less than a twentieth the size of America's at market exchange rates, the economic impact has been greater, but is still less than the rosy-eyed would like to claim.

But NAFTA has had wider effects, and these matter a lot more. Up to a point, these wider consequences were intended, and are welcome. The trade agreement has helped to make sure that Mexico sticks to its programme of reform, and has thereby done much to improve the prickly relations between America and Mexico. Not at all intended, however, and far less welcome, has been NAFTA'S effect on American trade policy in general. The treaty's enemies have managed to blame it, usually unfairly, for all manner of ills; and, largely as a result, America's trade policy has stalled.

The modest economic plus

Start with the economics. Could the cause of such prolonged and savage argument really matter so little? Yes, it could, at least in the United States.

One reason is that, compared with the elephantine American economy, Mexico's is a mouse. Only 117,000 Americans have signed up for the benefits offered to workers displaced by NAFTA. Compare that with the 1.5m who lose their jobs each year from factory closures, slack demand and corporate restructuring, and the 2.8m new jobs created each year in the United States. Economists at the Institute for International Economics, a Washington think-tank, point out that American direct investment in Mexico has averaged less than $3 billion a year since 1994, NAFTA'S first year. That is under 0.5% of American firms' total spending on plant and equipment.

Second, other things have had a bigger effect on trade flows between the United States and

---

ACTIVITY (Continued)

Mexico. Mexican exports to America have surged in the past two years, and trade in the opposite direction has slowed, chiefly because the peso's collapse in late 1994 and early 1995 made Mexican goods much cheaper in dollars, and American ones pricier in pesos. The currency crisis was the result of Mexican economic mismanagement. NAFTA, by promising a strong flow of investment, may have lulled the Mexicans into a false sense of security about the sustainability of the overvalued peso; but do not blame the pact itself.

Anyway, NAFTA was not the huge leap towards free trade that its champions said it would be. The United States already had low tariffs on most of its goods. It therefore did not need to liberalise its markets much; and, even when it did, some favoured sectors, such as agriculture, remained protected. Furthermore, Mexican trade liberalization had begun in the mid-1980s. In 1985, the country's business and political leaders, fed up after yet another economic crisis, abandoned decades of protectionism, joining GATT the following year. By 1990, Mexico's exports were 14% of its GDP, twice as much as ten years before. Although NAFTA took things further, cutting tariffs on American (and Canadian) goods from 10% to 3%, trade between Mexico and the United States was booming long before (see chart 1).

Ah, say NAFTA'S defenders, but what about Mexico's response to the peso crisis? In 1995 Mexico did not put up the shutters against foreign goods, as it had after the debt crisis of 1982. NAFTA kept it closer to the straight and narrow. This is true but NAFTA cannot take all the credit. As economists at the University of California at Los Angeles say in a recent study,[1] Mexico's economy had already become closely integrated with that of the United States as a result of the 1980s reforms. Mexican exporters had to import materials and components in order to make their wares. Curbing imports would merely have intensified Mexico's economic pain.

Does all this mean that NAFTA'S economic effects have been negligible? Not at all. It is a deal among only three countries, and by discriminating against others may have damagingly diverted some trade and investment. Some of Asia's textile and car trade with the United States seems to have been lost to Mexico, and the Caribbean and Central American countries are badgering America for "parity" with the Mexicans.

But there have been solid benefits, too; and the place to look for them is in Mexico more than in the United States. The change is not to be found in the maquiladoras, the duty-free assembly plants that sit along the American border, although their exports have risen by more than 18% a year since 1994. Within Mexico, both local and foreign manufacturers have been sprucing up their production, distribution and sales systems to equip themselves to supply an integrated North American market.

In the car industry, for instance, the twin forces of NAFTA and the peso crisis have made Mexico an attractive manufacturing centre for the whole region: exports of cars and trucks

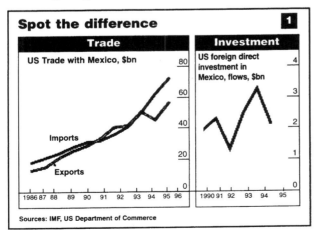

Spot the difference **1**

Trade — US Trade with Mexico, $bn — Imports — Exports — 1986 87 88 89 90 91 92 93 94 95 96

Investment — US foreign direct investment in Mexico, flows, $bn — 1990 91 92 93 94 95

Sources: IMF, US Department of Commerce

[1] Raul Hinojose Ojeda et al., *North American integration three years after NAFTA*. North American Integration and Development Centre. UCLA: December 1996.

ACTIVITY 3 (continued)

have doubled since 1994, to 1m units. Mexican firms whose suppliers provide second-rate material are spending a lot of money on training and financing local supplier networks. The textile-and-clothing business, says Gary Gereffi of Duke University, provides another example. In America, under pressure from Asian competitors. it had been in decline since the 1970s. The Mexican business was also in bad shape. Its protected manufacturers produced shoddy goods for local markets. Its *maquiladoras* worked for export, and used few local inputs.

Since the arrival of NAFTA, big firms in the southern United States and the north and centre of Mexico have been linking up. Manufacturers have been setting up joint ventures in Mexico which, unlike the *maquiladoras*, use local inputs: an example is the "textile city" project to be built near Mexico city by America's Guilford Mills and Dupont and Mexico's Grupo Alfa. And as big American retailers, such as Wal-Mart and Sears, have expanded their presence in Mexico, they are beginning to buy their branded clothes from Mexican plants, turning them from export-only *maquiladoras* into contract suppliers for the Mexican market. These big-name retailers are even starting to promote Mexican-made goods through their North American networks. The result of all these Mexican-American links, says MR. Gereffi, could be a North American textile-and clothing industry capable of taking on Asian rivals.

The biggest winners from this wave of investment and regional consolidation are likely to be ordinary Mexicans. They have long had to put up with tatty and/or expensive products manufactured by uncompetitive local firms. Tijuana is the world capital in television production; but television-buyers in Mexico City have until recently paid 10% more than Americans do. No longer. Mexicans can now buy a wider variety of things at lower prices, often with such once-unknown customer services as 24-hour free telephone numbers. Some pesticide makers

deliver their products to customers in northern Mexico directly from warehouses in Texas; firms in other industries do the reverse from warehouses in Mexico. Goods arrive faster and firms can cut back on inventories: a gain both for customers and for the companies themselves.

The bigger gain—and loss

Fine: but the consequences go deeper. It is in politics, not economics, that NAFTA has had its biggest impact. The trade agreement has come close, and perhaps irreversible, embrace between Mexico and the United States. Given the history of hostility between the two countries, this embrace is remarkable. Its cause was the realization by American officials that their chance of stemming the flow of illegal drugs and immigrants from Mexico would be far greater were their southern neighbours rich rather than poor. Freer trade and internal economic liberalization in Mexico were therefore to be encouraged.

American presidents are now prepared to defend Mexico against an often hostile Congress. In return, Mexican leaders have ditched their old gringo-bashing rhetoric. Richard Feinberg, formerly an adviser of Mr. Clinton's, says contentedly: "We bought ourselves an ally with NAFTA."

Two incidents have made clear the importance of the alliance both to Mr. Clinton and to the Mexicans. One came after the peso crisis broke in December 1994, sending Mexico's economy tumbling into the worst recession in Mexican memory. Mr. Clinton rushed in, putting together a $50 billion international rescue package against the objections of Congress. According to John Sweeney, an American Treasury official, the rescue would have been almost impossible without NAFTA.

ACTIVITY 3 (continued)

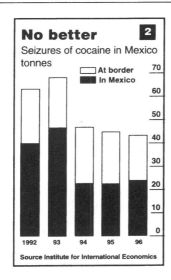

No better 2

Seizures of cocaine in Mexico
tonnes

☐ At border
■ In Mexico

1992 93 94 95 96

Source Institute for International Economics

The second illustration of the political by-products of NAFTA came this spring, when Mr. Clinton renewed Mexico's "certification" as a good comrade in the war against drugs. He did this despite the stream of drugs that still crosses America's southern border, and despite the arrest in February of Mexico's top anti-drug policeman on suspicion of being in the pay of drug barons.

Alas, NAFTA's effect on the United States has not been entirely benign. Mr. Clinton has admittedly been more or less free, despite grumblings in Congress, to continue his political love affair with Mexico: witness a pally visit to Mexico in May, which yielded deals on farm trade, drugs and immigration. But the continuing squabbles over the effect of NAFTA have blighted his efforts to push on with other trade-liberalisation deals. "The aftermath of the politics of NAFTA," says Fritz Mayer, ex-Congress staffman and another academic at Duke University, "has frozen American trade initiatives."

When NAFTA came into operation, this was almost unthinkable. In a televised debate in November 1993, Vice-President Al Gore wiped the floor with Ross Perot, billionaire businessman and protectionist presidential candidate,

who had famously forecast a "giant sucking sound" as American jobs vanished southwards. The same month, NAFTA squeaked through Congress. This helped to break down resistance to a far more important global trade agreement the Uruguay round of GATT talks in December. All seemed set fair for further trade initiatives. Bringing Chile into NAFTA, the planned first stage of extending the agreement to cover all the Americas except Cuba, looked a doddle.

Yet, despite NAFTA's modest economic effects in the United States and the health of that country's economy it grew by 4.1% in the year to the first quarter of 1997, unemployment is down to 4.8%, the lowest level since 1973, and inflation is 2.2% and falling the squabbling over NAFTA is as bitter as ever. As a result, in the second term of his presidency, Bill Clinton finds himself trying, without success, to win "fast-track" negotiating authority on trade from Congress, so that he can ask Congress to vote a straight yes or no to trade deals without fiddling amendments. Unless the president gets his way on this, other countries will remain chary of making deals with America that could later be modified by Congress. As a result, Chile is still waiting to start serious talks with America on its entry to NAFTA, although it has signed trade agreements with both Canada and Mexico.

Other things are having to wait, too. Mr. Clinton has been unable to promise much trade liberalisation in the Asia-Pacific Economic Cooperation forum. This is a retreat: in 1993, after a successful meeting of the forum's leaders in Seattle, he seemed to be the leader of a campaign to open up the Pacific. And in the past few months Mr. Clinton's hopes of swift agreement on China's entry into the World Trade Organisation have turned to dust, despite a House of Representatives vote in favour of continuing to treat China on equal terms with America's other trading partners.

Granted, there are plenty of other forces at

ACTIVITY 3 (continued)

work besides rows over NAFTA. Mr. Clinton's China policy has been tarnished by charges that the Democrats' coffers for last year's election campaign were swollen by Chinese cash. After swallowing both NAFTA and the Uruguay round in quick succession, America's lawmakers were inevitably suffering some trade indigestion. And it is no surprise that a Congress in Republican hands, as it has been since 1994, does not want to help a Democratic president.

But NAFTA's opponents have been doing their damnedest to give both the pact itself, and the whole notion of free trade a bad name. Freer trade they fear, means that Americans have to compete with workers in poorer countries who are willing, or are made, to work for far less pay and to put up with unsafe and unhealthy surroundings. Given the gap in pay and conditions, they say, American workers stand no chance. And free trade does not make only Americans miserable; it exploits the downtrodden foreigners, too.

NAFTA is an obvious target, because the competing paupers are on America's doorstep. Moreover, NAFTA's "side accords" intended to monitor labour conditions and safeguard the environment have proved toothless: Canada and Mexico accepted them only grudgingly, after much American lobbying, and insisted on making them hard to enforce. So Mexico City remains probably the world's filthiest big city, and border towns are sprawls of maquiladoras and sewage-filled rivers. Mexican trade unions have been kept in check for years by the ruling party, though this may change if the left does well in this Sunday's elections.

The peso crisis gave NAFTA's critics a double opportunity. America's rising trade deficit with Mexico made the administration's promises that NAFTA would boost American exports (and so, it claimed, employment) look hollow. And Mr. Clinton's rescue package for the peso, although it turned out to be a remarkable success made it easy for NAFTA's opponents to claim that the

United States had hitched itself to a deadbeat neighbor.

Another problem for NAFTA, says Mr. Mayer, has been "guilt by contagion: passing NAFTA made us closer to Mexico in some physical sense." Americans now look more sharply at Mexico than they did before NAFTA, and they do not like everything they see. Some see an open door to trade as little different from an open door to illegal drugs and illegal immigration, even though there is no reason why NAFTA should increase either. To add fuel to the argument, the recession south of the border has led Mexicans to try slipping into the United States in even greater numbers.

Just say yes

Worst of all for Mr. Clinton, perhaps, Americans' misgivings about trade are being

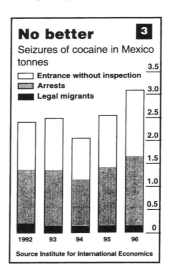

No better ▪3
Seizures of cocaine in Mexico
tonnes
☐ Entrance without inspection
▨ Arrests
■ Legal migrants

1992 93 94 95 96

Source Institute for International Economics

articulated not just by isolated hotheads in Congress and the labour movement but also by Richard Gephardt, the Democrats' leader in the House. Mr. Gephardt wants to succeed Mr. Clinton as president. The president would rather the job went to Mr. Gore.

And therein lies the rub. Mr. Gore, both as Mr. Clinton's number two and as Mr. Perot's demolisher, is linked with the passage of

ACTIVITY 3 (continued)

NAFTA. Mr. Gephardt, who in 1993 voted against NAFTA, insists there should be no new fast-track authority without negotiations on labor and environmental standards. The Republicans want no such conditions. If Mr. Clinton, who has said he will ask for negotiating authority again in September, wants a fast-track mandate, he will probably have to lean towards the Republicans. That would pit him, and Mr. Gore, directly against Mr. Gephardt.

As an old friend of the labour movement, Mr. Gephardt is doing these things out of conviction as well as opportunism. But the effect on Mr. Clinton's trade policy is the same, whatever Mr. Gephardt's motives. The president must forgo progress on trade, or risk scuppering Mr. Gore's chances of the White House.

For the United States, the best thing would be to snub the trade-union and green lobbies and press on with trade liberalisation. The brief history of NAFTA indicates that America has nothing to fear from trade with poorer countries; indeed, it has lots to gain from freer trade on a much wider scale. And freer trade would also be best for the developing countries. They would not only get richer, and be able to buy more American goods; in time, their working conditions and the state of their environment would improve, too, as their growing middle class insisted on the right to a cleaner and more comfortable life.

Thanks in part to NAFTA, this is the prospect in Mexico. And, as Mr. Clinton realises, a prosperous Mexico is more likely to keep its sons and daughters at home, and see fewer of them become illegal immigrants or drug smugglers. That would please people on both sides of the border.

ACTIVITY 4
TAKING SIDES: ASSESSMENT

Tell whether each of the following groups would be for or against NAFTA; explain your answers. If you think that group's opinion could go either way, explain that as well.

A. U.S. Trade unions

B. Mexican consumers

C. Environmentalists

D. Asian textile manufacturers

E. The American and Mexican textile and clothing business

F. The country of Chile

PRIVATIZATION AROUND THE WORLD

INTRODUCTION

In the past decade, privatization initiatives have been widely used in developed market economies, in developing nations, and in the transition economies that were part of the former Soviet bloc. Individual manufacturing enterprises and entire industries, once owned by the state, have been turned over to private control and ownership under these programs. So too have a wide range of services that have traditionally been provided by the public sector. For example, some countries have privatized prisons, schools, hospitals, postal services, and even Social Security programs.

Several different approaches have been used to privatize state-owned enterprises and social programs, and the results of privatization have been much more successful in some countries and cases than in others. Those approaches and some international comparisons of the results of privatization are presented in this lesson.

The underlying idea in all of the privatization initiatives is that private ownership will establish profit incentives and greater competition that, together, will result in more efficient operation of enterprises and greater responsiveness to consumer or taxpayer preferences.

CONCEPTS

Incentives
Competition
Institutions
Property rights
Privatization

CONTENT STANDARDS

Institutions evolve in market economies to help individuals and groups accomplish their goals. Banks, labor unions, corporations, legal systems, and not-for-profit organizations are examples of important institutions. A different kind of institution, clearly defined and enforced property rights, is essential to a market economy.

Different methods can be used to allocate goods and services. People acting individually or collectively through government must choose which methods to use for allocating goods and services.

Property rights, contract enforcement, standards for weights and measures, and liability rules affect incentives for people to produce and exchange goods and services.

Competition among sellers lowers costs and prices and encourages producers to produce more of what consumers are willing and able to buy.

OBJECTIVES

◆ Explain the relationship between clearly defined private property rights and incentives to use resources efficiently today and in the future.

◆ Analyze the advantages and disadvantages of four alternative approaches to privatization: restitution, sales to outside (foreign) owners, management-employee buyouts, and public voucher programs.

◆ Compare results from successful and unsuccessful privatization programs used in many different developing and transition economies, and discuss the long-term consequences of those differing results.

LESSON DESCRIPTION

In this lesson, students review and evaluate the approaches most widely used to privatize public enterprises and services. They also review some international comparisons on the success of these programs in different nations. In the assessment section, references to several articles on privatization that have appeared in recent issues of *The Economist* magazine are provided to enable teachers and students to learn more about specific examples of privatization programs in many different countries and industries.

TIME REQUIRED

One or two class periods.

MATERIALS

★ One transparency each for Visuals 1-4, or copies to distribute to students

★ One copy of Activity 1 for each student

PROCEDURE

1. Ask students to give examples of both private property and public property. *(Suggested examples include: Private property: the clothes students are wearing, cars they or their parents own, most houses and apartment buildings in the United States, food in their homes or for sale in grocery stores, and all privately-owned businesses. Public property: most government buildings (including courthouses, police and fire stations, administrative and legislative buildings), public parks, military bases and equipment, and most elementary and secondary school buildings in this country.)*

2. Ask students to list the key characteristics of public and private property. After some discussion, display a transparency of Visual 1 or distribute copies to students. Review the ideas in the transparency, using specific examples of private property such as a family that decides to rent out a spare room or to start up a new business. Contrast that with examples of publicly-owned property, such as the original copy of the U.S. Constitution or a public park. *(The idea of individual vs. government ownership is fine as a starting point, but be sure to stress the two key functional ideas of property rights: 1) the right to exclude others from using the property, and 2) the right to transfer the property to others as a gift or an exchange.)*

3. Discuss with students the key incentives associated with private property, namely that the private owners will bear any costs of maintaining the property as long as they own it, but they will reap the rewards obtained from the use of the property, too. That gives individuals stronger personal incentives to take care of things they own, while publicly-owned resources are often abused by those who use them. Ask

students to discuss examples of these problems. *(In extreme cases, publicly-owned resources [such as the buffalo and whales] nearly faced extinction, and others have become extinct, because no one owned these resources and thus nobody had incentives to use them carefully. Instead, those who hunted these animals were trying to get as many for themselves as possible, before someone else got them. Not at all the same incentives as, say, those that a cattle rancher or a wheat farmer faces in this country. Less extreme examples include more litter in public areas than in private homes and yards, pollution occurring in publicly-owned air and water, and efficiency problems in large government agencies that face no private competition and no "bottom line" profit-or- loss financial constraints.)*

4. Explain that in many countries in recent decades governments have been privatizing many different goods and services that were formerly produced by state-owned enterprises. Some highways, prisons, hospitals, and schools have been privatized in the U.S. Steel and other large industries once nationalized under Labour governments in the U.K. have been privatized. In Chile, there is a promising experiment underway with a privatized Social Security program. Many other examples are discussed in the articles listed in the **Assessment** section of this lesson. Review the reasons for such initiatives, including the incentive effects of private ownership and the competitive pressures that face private firms in the marketplace.

5. Explain that the most extensive privatization initiatives in the past decade have occurred in the developing economies and, not surprisingly, in the transition economies that were part of the former Soviet bloc. In those countries, four main ways have been used to privatize enterprises. Distribute Activity 1 to the class and divide the class into four groups. Assign each group to study one of the privatization options in Activity 1. Ask the students to identify various forms of privatization. Summarize the available forms by displaying Visual 2. After students have com-

pleted their discussion, display Visual 3. Ask the class to analyze the options. Place a "plus" in the chart if the objective is fulfilled by a given method and a "minus" if it is not. Use a question mark if the outcome is uncertain. *(Suggested answers follow.)*

			Objectives		
Methods	Better corporate governance	Speed	Better access to capital and skills	More government revenue	Greater fairness
Restitution	?	–	?	–	+
Sales to outside owners	+	–	+	+	?
Management-employee buyouts	–	+	–	–	–
Equal access voucher privatization	?	+	?	–	+

6. Explain that economists have studied privatization programs in different countries, classifying them as successful, moderately successful, or unsuccessful, based mainly on two criteria: a) the scope or amount of assets that have been privatized, and b) the stability of such initiatives over periods of 5 years or longer. Once countries were classified using these criteria, data on foreign direct investment and other privatization revenues were calculated for the three different groups. Display Visual 4 to show that foreign direct investment and other privatization revenues were much higher in the successful privatizing countries than in the unsuccessful countries. Discuss how that investment should help these countries grow much faster in the future. As an extension activity, you can assign small groups of students to study individual countries from these three categories and have them report on the privatization programs they learn about, using *The Economist* or other financial and news magazines or newspapers as sources.

ASSESSMENT

Have students read and report on any of the following sources: the articles from *The Economist*, listed below; the special insert on privatization in the October 2, 1995, issue of the *Wall Street Journal*, titled "Sale of the Century"; or similar articles from these or other publications. Be sure students stress the concepts and issues covered in this lesson.

From *The Economist*:

Argentina, "Privatisation, It's Fairly Wonderful," January 8, 1994, p. 42.

Brazil, "A Shiny Future," November 5, 1994, pp. 68-69; "Privatisation Trundles Ahead," June 15, 1996, p. 42.

Canada, "All Aboard," September 2, 1995, pp. 58-59.

Czech Republic, "A Private Matter, " May 28, 1994, p. 50.

El Salvador and Chile, "Fast Lane and Slow," March 23, 1996.

France, "Pusillanimous Privatisation," September 17, 1994, p. 73; "The State is Dead: Long Live the State," November 25, 1995, pp. 12-14; "Privatisation Takes French Leave," December 9, 1995, pp. 59-60; "Xenophobia, Meet Myopia," December 7, 1997, pp. 58-59.

Ghana, "Golden Shares," March 19, 1994, p. 96.

India, "Disconnected," May 7, 1994, pp. 86-87.

Italy, "The Price of Privatisation," May 3, 1997, pp. 66-67.

Nigeria, "Privatisation? Forget It," January 25, 1997, pp. 41-42.

Peru, "A Shinier Path?" February 5, 1994, p. 70.

Poland, "Not There Yet," September 3, 1994, pp. 52-53.

Russia, "Not the Real Thing Yet," March 12, 1994, p. 58; "Disputes are Forever," September 17, 1994, pp. 73-74; "Psst! Want to Buy a Country?" November 5, 1994, p. 64; "Who Will Buy Russia?" September 9, 1995, pp. 73-74; "As You Were," January 6, 1996, pp. 54-55.

South Africa, "Looking for Hush Money," March 6, 1995, pp. 66-67.

Spain, "Compañias Españolas," December 14, 1996, pp. 9-10.

Tanzania, "Private-sector Beer is Best," November 2, 1996, p. 46.

Ukraine, "Reformers Anonymous," September 2, 1995, pp. 48-49.

U.K., "Bewitched, Bothered and Bewildered," July 16, 1994, pp. 49, 52; "How to Privatize," March 11, 1995, pp. 16-17; "The Thatcher Revolution," September 21, 1996, pp. 8-11.

U.S., "From Highway to My Way," November 18, 1995, pp. 29-30.

U.S. and U.K., "The State and Real Estate," August 31, 1996, p. 18.

VISUAL 1

What Are Property Rights?

Property rights include the right to:

- Use property you own as you see fit (subject to zoning restrictions and other laws establishing illegal uses).

- Receive any income created by the use of property you own.

- Permit or exclude others from using property you own.

- Sell or transfer property you own to others.

- Use the legal system to enforce your property rights if someone takes or uses your property without your permission.

Forms of Privatization

- Restitution

- Sales to outside owners (including foreign owners)

- Management - employee buyouts

- Equal access voucher sales

Advantages and Disadvantages of
Privatization Alternatives

Methods	Better corporate governance	Speed	Objectives Better access to capital and skills	More government revenue	Greater fairness
Restitution					
Sales to outside owners					
Management-employee buyouts					
Equal access voucher privatization					

VISUAL 4

Successful Privatization and Foreign Direct Investment Inflows

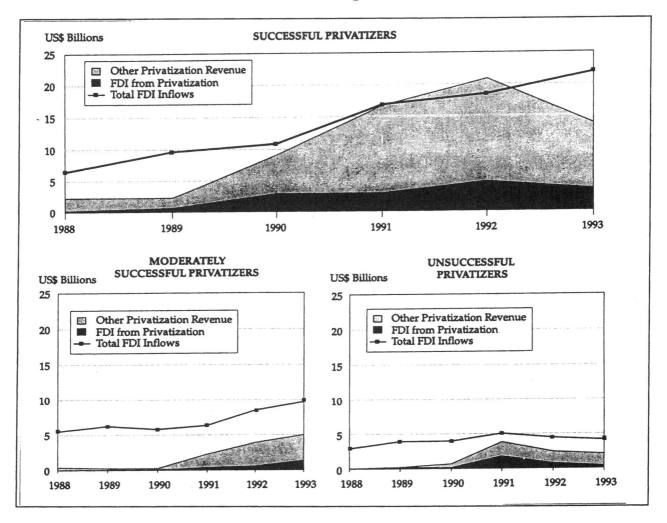

Note: "Successful Privatizers" includes: Argentina, Chile, Czech Republic, Hungary, Jamaica, Malaysia, Mexico, the Philippines, and Portugal. "Moderately Successful Privatizers" includes: Barbados, Benin, Brazil, Estonia, Ghana, Honduras, Indonesia, Laos, Morocco, Nicaragua, Nigeria, Pakistan, Peru, Poland, Sri Lanka, Thailand, Togo, and Tunisia. "Unsuccessful Privatizers" includes: Bangladesh, Bolivia, Bulgaria, Colombia, Cote d'Ivoire, Egypt, Greece, India, Kenya, Lithuania, Mozambique, Nepal, Romania, Turkey, Uganda, Ukraine, Uruguay, Venezuela, Viet Nam, and Zambia.

Source: *Facilitating Foreign Participation in Privatization,* Foreign Investment Advisory Service of the International Finance Corporation and the World Bank, 1996, p. 6.

ACTIVITY 1
APPROACHES TO PRIVATIZATION

Directions: Read the options below, as assigned by your teacher, and identify their advantages and disadvantages. Be prepared to present your ideas as part of a group discussion.

Over the centuries market economics have developed laws that govern rights to property ownership. The existence of private property is commonplace in the United States, England, and many other countries. In most of the transition economies in eastern Europe and the former Soviet Union, however, state ownership of property has been the norm until recently. Today, each of the transition economies is seeking the best means to transfer ownership of state property into private hands. After decades of central planning, the problems are very real. How can state enterprises be transferred to private ownership?

Option 1: Restitution

Restitution means returning property to former owners who can show clear property ownership claims. A clear claim, for example, might involve presenting documents to show that you were the last owner of a farm before collectivization. Many people in the nations of Eastern Europe and the Baltics enjoyed private ownership until 1945, and some of them still can show documentation of ownership. Bulgaria, the Czech Republic, and Slovenia have passed laws providing for restitution of land, housing, and enterprises. Estonia, Latvia, and Lithuania have passed laws providing for restitution of urban and rural land.

Advantages of restitution

A primary advantage of restitution is that it restores property to those from whom it was taken. Restitution has often been used successfully in cases involving smaller firms and farms. In cases where restitution is not a practical means of restoring ownership, other forms of

repayment have been made to past owners. In Hungary, for example, previous owners have been compensated with coupons which represent value in private firms and can be traded on stock markets.

Disadvantages of restitution

Restitution has its limits. Prior ownership is often hard to prove. Many properties such as large state enterprises may never have had private owners, or may have been extensively developed with later public investments. When small properties such as housing or apartments are returned, disputes may result because existing tenants believe they also have rights. Arguments over restitution claims may slow the process of moving some properties into private hands. Finally, because it involves no sale of government-owned property, restitution provides little or no new government revenue.

Option 2: Sales to outside owners

This method involves selling state enterprises on a case-by-case basis to people other than the current managers and employees. In many transition economies, the sales have included sales to foreign investors. This model has worked in the transition economies and in some Western European nations (the United Kingdom, for example).

Advantages of sales to outside owners

A potential advantage is that such sales can turn enterprises over to people with the knowledge, skill, and resources needed to run them successfully. Foreign investors often bring new ideas for corporate governance. Sales to outside owners also increase government revenue.

Disadvantages of sales to outside owners

In practice, sales to outside owners have moved slowly, and only a few large firms have been privatized in this fashion. The sheer size

Source: Adapted from *From Plan to Market: Ideas for Social Studies, Economics, and Business Classes*, National Council on Economic Education, 1997.

ACTIVITY 1 (continued)

of the job contributes to the problem. Negotiations take time. Moreover, inadequate accounting rules and the lack of a price structure have made it difficult to know what an enterprise is actually worth. Finally, many citizens have felt that such sales are unfair because typical citizens are unable to participate in the process. Sales to foreign owners are sometimes politically unpopular.

Option 3: Management-employee buyouts

Management-employee buyouts involve the purchase of an enterprise by the existing management and employees. Such buyouts have been widely used in Croatia, Poland, Romania, Slovenia, and Russia. Many firms privatized through voucher programs effectively became management-employee buyouts, as employees and their families used vouchers and cash to buy major shares in the firms.

Disadvantages of management-employee buyouts

There are several problems. The benefits are unequally distributed because people in good firms get good assets while those in money-losers get little or nothing of value. Others who are not employed at all, such as pensioners, receive nothing. Most important, management-employee buyouts do not guarantee that the current managers are capable. No new skills or capital are acquired. Managers in the transition economies were trained to meet old incentives production quotas not to be responsive to consumers. In other words, things may not change very much under this system.

Option 4: Equal access voucher privatization

A fourth form of privatization distributes vouchers or ownership shares across the population and attempts to allocate assets evenly among voucher holders. Mongolia, Lithuania, and the Czech Republic were the first countries to implement this form of privatization. Poland and Russia followed. The mass privatization

program in the Czech Republic has been the most successful. In two successive waves, the Czechs transferred half the assets of state enterprises into private hands. Citizens were free to invest their vouchers directly in the firms being auctioned. However, people also could pool their vouchers to acquire ownership shares in large firms. More than two-thirds of the voucher holders chose to place their vouchers in such pools or mutual funds.

Advantages of equal access voucher privatization

Such programs excel in speed, and in public popularity, due to their perceived fairness. The experience in the Czech Republic shows that such programs help develop capital markets and quickly create stakeholders with an interest in reform.

Disadvantages of equal access voucher privatization

Such programs offer little or no new government revenue. They do not guarantee that new managers will be capable. It is uncertain if new skills or capital will be acquired. Finally, the trading of vouchers depends upon access to financial markets, such as stock markets, banks, and mutual funds. Such markets are well established in mature market economies, where there are rules regarding financial responsibility and disclosure. The transition economies, however, have not yet developed such systems.

CATCHING UP OR FALLING BEHIND? INTERNATIONAL COMPARISONS OF NATIONAL INCOME AND ECONOMIC GROWTH

INTRODUCTION

Among the industrialized nations of the world, there is a clear, long-standing trend for income levels to converge towards the income level in the industrialized nation that currently has the highest level of income in the world. Sometimes nations even surpass the nation that previously had the highest level of income. For example, the United States and several other countries have now passed the United Kingdom, which had the highest level of per capita income or gross domestic product (GDP) in the world through most of the nineteenth century. This happened even though income levels in the United Kingdom continued to rise in absolute terms.

Through the twentieth century, the United States has enjoyed the world's highest levels of per capita GDP. Since World War II, however, many industrialized nations, including Germany and Japan, have been catching up rapidly, and some (such as France and Italy) may soon surpass U.S. income levels.

This lesson introduces this idea of convergence in income levels over time, presenting the major reasons economists have identified to explain why such convergence occurs. The lesson also deals with the conflicting idea of divergence in income levels between industrialized and less developed nations, and briefly examines reasons why that has occurred.

CONCEPTS

National income (GDP per capita)
Productivity
Saving
Investments in physical and human capital
Diminishing returns to capital
International capital flows
Technology transfers

CONTENT STANDARDS

Investment in factories, machinery, new technology, and the health, education, and training of people can raise future standards of living.

Gross Domestic Product (GDP) is a basic measure of a nation's economic output and income. It is the total market value, measured in dollars or some other currency, of all final goods and services produced in the economy in one year.

Per capita GDP is GDP divided by the number of people living in a country.

Productivity is measured by dividing output (goods and services) by the number of inputs used to produce the output.

Standards of living increase as the productivity of labor increases.

Investments in physical and human capital can increase productivity, but such investments entail opportunity costs and economic risks.

When the quantity of one or more inputs is increased, while at least one input remains fixed, the amount of additional output produced by using additional units of the variable input(s) will eventually begin to decrease.

Technological change is an advance in knowledge leading to new and improved goods and services and better ways of producing them.

OBJECTIVES

◆ Understand historical evidence on the convergence of income and output levels for industrialized market economies, and the divergence of income and output levels in those nations compared to less developed nations.

◆ Analyze reasons why industrialized nations tend to "catch up" to output and income levels for other industrialized nations that have higher levels of output and income.

◆ Identify some of the reasons why income levels in less developed nations have grown more slowly than income levels in the industrialized market economies.

LESSON DESCRIPTION

Student teams participate in several rounds of a production simulation to discover the causes of convergence in output and income levels in industrialized nations. Before the simulation, they examine historical evidence on these patterns of convergence. After the simulation, they see historical evidence on the divergence between output and income levels in industrialized and less developed nations, and consider reasons for that divergence.

TIME REQUIRED

One or two class periods.

MATERIALS

★ 300 sheets of 8½ x 11" white paper
★ 50 sheets each of paper in two colors other than white
★ Eight pairs of scissors
★ Six glue sticks
★ Four jars of rubber cement
★ Four rulers with metal strips on one edge
★ 250 one dollar bills copied from Activity 1 (optional)
★ Copies of Visuals 1, 3, and 4 for each student and/or an overhead transparency for each
★ A transparency for Visual 2

PROCEDURE

1. **Brainstorming and background.** Ask students to state or write down the country in which they believe people have the highest level of annual income. Write their answers on the board or an overhead transparency. Then display Visual 1 on an overhead projector, or distribute a copy of it to each student. Explain that GDP is a basic measure of a nation's annual income, measured by how many final goods and services are produced and are therefore available for people to consume. Per capita GDP is GDP divided by the number of people in the country, so it is a basic measure of the average income of people in the country. Ask whether the students are surprised by the relative position for the United States shown in Visual 1, or by the pattern that shows the other nations catching up to U.S. levels of income. Have the students suggest ideas about why the other nations have been catching up. Then announce that the class will participate in several rounds of a simulation to illustrate some of the reasons for the convergence.

2. **Group assignments.** Divide the class into two groups, representing factories in the mythical countries of Mesaros and Suiterland. Appoint a management team of three students for each factory. Have the management groups choose five other people to work in the factory in their country. NOTE WELL: USE THE SAME TEAMS OF WORKERS AND MANAGERS IN ALL OF THE FOLLOWING PROCEDURES, TO ILLUSTRATE THE EFFECTS OF CHANGING CAPITAL RESOURCES WHILE HOLDING LABOR AND MANAGEMENT INPUTS CONSTANT.

3. **Distributing materials.** The factories in both countries will produce "Gadgets," which are described below, made with the following materials. Give both groups a ruler (preferably one with a metal edge) and a large stack of 8 1/2" by 11" white paper. (It doesn't matter if the paper has been used or written on before, but it must be smooth and easy to fold and stack neatly). Also give each group 10 sheets of paper that is some color other than white, and five sheets of paper that is a third color. (Construction paper is fine, but not necessary.) Give the team from Mesaros, but not the team from Suiterland, a pair of scissors and a glue stick. Give the team from Suiterland, but not the team from Mesaros, a container of rubber cement.

4. **What's a gadget?** Demonstrate to all the students how to produce a Gadget. Cut one

piece of white paper in half so that you end up with two pieces that are 8½" wide and approximately 5¾" tall. Warn the students that if the white paper is more than 6" tall or less than 5" tall, it can not be used to produce an acceptable Gadget. Assign one student to serve as an inspector, and give this student a ruler to measure the height of white sheets after a Gadget has been completely produced. To complete the production of the Gadget, have students cut or tear out 1" squares, using the two colored sheets of paper. Cement or glue four squares of one color in each of the four corners of the Gadget, and three squares of the other color in a straight-line solid rectangle that crosses the midpoint of the Gadget, either horizontally or vertically. Tell the inspector to reject any Gadget that is too tall or too short, or that does not have the proper number and arrangement of colored squares.

5. Producing gadgets: Round one.

Assemble each group of production workers around a desk or table. Give the two teams of students 2½ minutes to produce as many Gadgets as they can. If one or both groups seem(s) uncertain about how to produce Gadgets, stop the round to explain and demonstrate the procedure again, remove all of the completed or partially completed Gadgets, make sure the teams have enough paper, and then restart the round, allowing 2½ minutes for production. When the production period is completed, have the inspector check each complete Gadget and discard any that are not properly made, as well as any that were only partially completed. Record the production levels for both factories/countries on the chalkboard or an overhead transparency.

6. Linking productivity and income.

Announce that Gadgets are sold worldwide for a price that is equivalent to $2, and pay each management group $2 for each Gadget their factory made that was approved by the inspector. (Either distribute dollar bills copied from Activity 1, or just have the management teams and, later, individual students keep ledgers indicating their dollar balance.) Collect those

Gadgets and dispose of them, too. Explain that in this simulation, for simplicity, we assume that Gadgets are the only final product (i.e., a product not used as an input to produce something else) made in each country, so this income represents the economy's GDP. Announce that from the money received by each management team, they must now pay 20 percent as taxes (paid to the teacher). Then they must pay an additional 20 percent (also to the teacher) for the raw materials (paper, glue or rubber cement, etc.) used in the production. They must pay 50 percent to the workers. The remaining 10 percent can be kept by the management team, or it may be reinvested in the factory to purchase additional capital for use in later production rounds.

7. Investing in capital goods.

Before beginning the second round, announce that either management team may buy as many pairs of scissors as it wants for $2 each, or as many glue sticks as it likes for $1 each, as many containers of rubber cement as it likes for 50 cents each, and as many rulers as it likes for 50 cents each. These capital goods will be for use in any future rounds, and the management teams may continue to use the capital goods they started with in round one. Announce that the percentage charges they pay for raw materials (paper), labor, and taxes will remain the same in all rounds. Show these charges and the prices for any capital goods the factories may want to purchase at this time, using Visual 2.

Allow time for the management teams to discuss their options. If it happens that either team decides to try to borrow money from its workers to purchase capital items, allow that to happen, but do not suggest it at this time. If it does happen, limit the amount that workers can lend to 20 percent of their wages, as described below in procedure 10. In this round, do not allow either country to provide funds for investment to the other country. Let the teams make their capital purchases. As long as one team purchases something, proceed with the second production round. If neither team makes a capital purchase, encourage both teams to reconsider that. If necessary say that you will provide a loan to one or both countries to purchase at least one additional unit of capital. Explain that you will lend these funds but expect to be repaid at the end of the next round with 10 percent interest per round. Once some capital has been purchased, begin round 2.

8. **Producing gadgets: Round two.** Once again, give the two factories $2^{1}/_{2}$ minutes to produce as many Gadgets as they can, have the inspector check each complete Gadget, and discard any that are not properly made. Record the production levels for both factories/countries on the chalkboard or an overhead transparency, next to the production results for round one. Pay each management group $2 for each Gadget their factory made that was approved by the inspector. Collect those Gadgets and dispose of them, too.

9. **First debriefing.** Production levels should have been higher in round two in any country that purchased additional capital. Students should see that the additional capital goods allow the workers to be more productive, so production levels, GDP, and the factory and workers' incomes will all rise. Point out that if the Suiterland group was able to purchase scissors or a glue stick, then they are not only adding to their stock of capital goods, but also importing a new and better technology that was not available to them in the first round. That also increases productivity. If one group did not purchase additional capital for the second round, it is still possible that production for that factory increased, because the workers were more experienced and perhaps better organized in producing Gadgets. It is unlikely, however, that output would increase as much for that group as for the group that purchased additional capital.

10. **Linking saving and investment.** If it has not happened before, announce that the management teams can borrow money from the workers to purchase additional capital. That would be in the workers' interests, too, because their wages payments increase when the factories' production levels increase. However, limit

the amount any worker can lend to 20 percent of his or her wages in the previous round. Explain that this limit reflects the fact that workers must purchase food, housing, clothing, transportation, medical and educational services, and pay taxes. Money they lend to the management team is a form of saving, which is used to finance additional investments in capital goods. Any profit that the management teams uses to purchase additional capital goods is also a form of saving (specifically, retained earnings).

11. **Producing gadgets, round three.** Conduct another production round, as described above in Procedure 8.

12. **Second debriefing.** Additional capital investments will probably continue to increase total production, but perhaps not as much as earlier purchases of capital goods in a given factory/country. If diminishing returns to capital investments do appear in the results, either debrief that now, as discussed below in Procedure 13, or hold that discussion until after the fourth production round. In either case, note that more capital goods increase total output of Gadgets and income levels.

In debriefing rounds, explain that this simulation is different from the real world because it holds labor and other resources except capital constant. Most countries actually experienced large increases in labor resources throughout the last century. The diminishing returns to capital illustrated in this lesson were never directly observed in countries with fixed labor or other resources. Instead, those effects were statistically estimated by economists, who measured the impact of increased capital investments in different countries after accounting for changes in labor and other resources. Doing that shows that diminishing returns to capital constitute an important reason for economic growth in countries catching up to the United States in this period, but there were other factors at work, too, that offset some of those effects in some ways. For example, good investment opportunities, high interest rates, and political stability in the United States led many foreigners to invest capital here during this period. And compared to the developing nations, more favorable investment climates in the industrialized nations contributed to the growing difference in income and production levels in the industrialized and developing nations.

13. **Additional production rounds.** Run as many rounds as it takes to show diminishing returns to capital. That may begin to happen in both groups in the same round, but it is more likely to occur first, and more severely, in the Meszaros group. Once it has appeared, explain the concept of diminishing returns to the entire class: as more units of an input are used in a production process, holding at least one input constant, eventually the increases in output will begin to decline. In this case, the number of workers was fixed, and as they had more and more capital to work with, the labor resource was spread more and more thinly across the available capital inputs. When this happens at an uneven rate in different countries, the capital owners have incentives to move capital resources to countries where capital is less plentiful and more productive.

14. **International capital investments and flows.** Before the final production round, let the Mesaros management group merge or simply take control of the Suiterland factory, and note that this has happened all over the world in recent years as U.S. companies have bought or built factories in other countries, and other countries have bought or built factories in the United States. The management team should then decide where to invest additional capital (scissors and glue sticks), and should choose to do that where production has been lagging due to lower capital investments. If the Mesaros team does not see the advantages of doing this, discuss the advantages of doing so with them and the entire class.

15. **Final production round.** Conduct the last production round, as described above in procedure eight.

16. **Final debriefing on convergence.** Distribute copies of Visual 3 to students, or display a copy they can see on an overhead projector. Note that the first three reasons listed for why per capita GDP converges in industrialized market economies (technology transfer, diminishing returns to capital, and international capital flows) were illustrated in the simulation. The other two reasons listed in Visual 3 were not shown in the simulation, but are reasonably intuitive and easy to understand. Research and development improves the quality of capital; and when technological progress is gradual, then technology transfer to countries that begin with older forms of capital will result in faster convergence. Put differently, under these conditions technology transfer combined with the gradual innovations resulting from research and development will lead to convergence, because it is typically cheaper to imitate and implement a known technology than it is to innovate and find a new technology. However, if technological progress is rapid and occurring primarily in the country that is already wealthiest and most productive, that can work against convergence, at least for a time. Education and training increase human capital, or the skills and productivity of workers. In countries where workers are well educated and trained, additional investments in physical capital such as factories and machines prove to be especially productive, so it is more likely that investments will be made in countries where the level of education and training is high.

17. **Debriefing on divergence especially in third world nations.** Distribute copies of Visual 3 to students, or display a copy they can see on an overhead projector. Given the earlier evidence and discussion on why industrialized nations tend to experience convergence in levels of income and productivity, ask students to discuss why the poorest nations seem to be falling farther and farther behind the living standards achieved in the most industrialized nations. One relevant factor illustrated in the simulation is differences in the saving rate of rich and poor countries. If wealthier nations save more than poorer ones, that will make capital investments

more likely to occur in the wealthy nations, raising productivity and income levels there faster than in poor nations. Among the industrialized nations, it often happens that nations not among the wealthiest save more than some wealthy nations — e.g., the rate of saving has been higher in Japan and Germany than in the United States, partly because tax laws and other policies make saving more attractive in those nations.

But saving is higher in virtually all of the industrialized nations than in very poor nations, and this contributes to divergence. Differences in population growth rates have also led to divergence, despite the fact that the growth rate of output (GDP) not adjusted for population growth has been faster in many developing nations than in industrialized nations over the past few decades. Finally, many of the Third World nations have been subject to political and economic instabilities, including government coups, wars, droughts or floods, bank failures or other financial crises, and legal barriers to international trade and investment. Those instabilities and restrictions have limited both domestic and international investment in these countries. Similar instabilities have, at times, resulted in countries that

were once among the wealthiest and most powerful in the word (such as ancient Greece, Rome, and Egypt; Spain in the 16th century; Argentina in the early decades of the 20th century; and the USSR in the late 1980s and early 1990s) to experience sharp drops in national output and income levels.

ASSESSMENT

1. Following the simulation, distribute a copy of Visuals 1, 3, and 4 to the students, and ask them to write a one- or two-page essay to discuss why the industrialized, high-income nations tend to converge toward the nation with the highest level of income, while poorer, less developed nations have tended to be left farther behind.

2. Ask the students or small groups of students to select specific nations or regions of several nations, and to investigate whether those nations and regions converged or diverged with the most industrialized nations in the world during the past two centuries. A similar assignment can be done for specific regions of the United States e.g., did the "Sunbelt" and "Rustbelt" states converge or diverge? Have the students prepare a short report to present to the class.

I. Trends in National Income (per capita GDP), 1870-1990

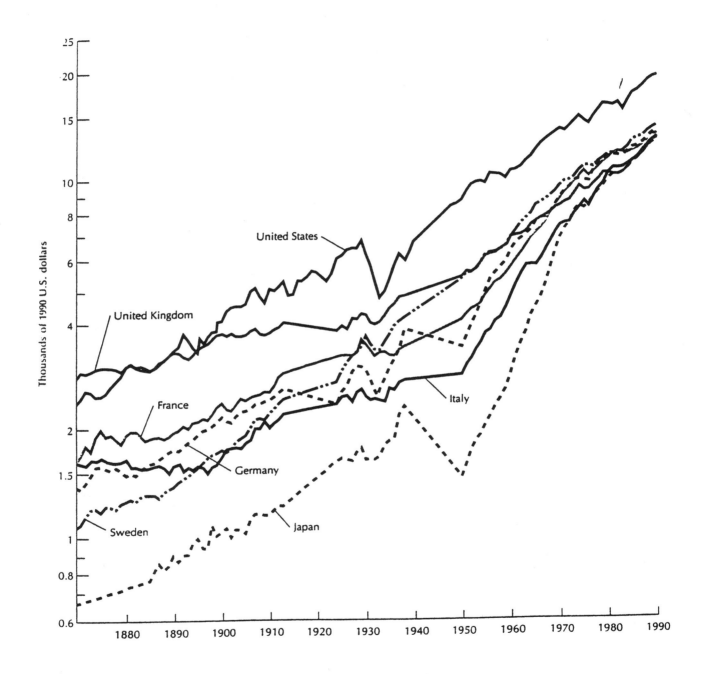

Source: Robert Gordon, *Macroeconomics*, 3rd Edition, p. 349.

VISUAL 1 (Continued)

II. Per Capita GDP* in Advanced Countries, Relative to the United States (%)

Country	GDP/Capita 1991	Productivity, GDP/Employees	GDP/Employee Projected to the Year 2000
United States	100	100	100
Japan	87	78	93
Germany	89	90	93
France	83	96	105
United Kingdom	74	76	80
Italy	77	96	104
Canada	89	89	90

*Comparisons based on OECD estimates of purchasing power parity exchange rates.

Source: Richard Freeman, ed., *Working Under Different Rules*, Russell Sage Foundation, New York, 1994, p. 9.

Costs and Revenues from Gadget Sales

Revenues: $2 for each compete Gadget produced and accepted by the Quality Control Inspection.

Costs: 20% Taxes

20% Raw Materials

50% Labor

Profits: 10%

Prices for Additional Capital Goods*

Scissors	$2 each
Glue Sticks	$1 each
Rubber Cement	$.50 each
Rulers	$.50 each

*Capital goods purchased in any round may be used in all future rounds.

Why Does Per Capita GDP Converge in Industrialized Market Economies?

1) Technology Transfer — Nations Copy Successful Innovations From the Wealthiest Nation

2) Diminishing Returns to Capital — Investments in Factories and Equipment Increase Output More in Countries That Have Less Capital

3) International Capital Flows — Capital Owners in the Nation with the Highest Income Support Capital Investments in Other Countries

4) Research and Development — Increases Output and Income, and when Technological Progress is Gradual and Widespread, This Can Help Other Nations Catch Up with the Richest Nation

5) Education and Training — Investments in Human Capital Increase Productivity Gains Resulting from Investments in Physical Capital (Factories and Equipment), Which Speeds the Flow of Capital Goods From the Richest Nation

Source: Adapted from Robert J. Barro and Xavier Sala-i-Martin, *Economic Growth*, McGraw-Hill, Inc., New York, 1995, pp. 265-266.

VISUAL 4

The Growing Divergence of Income Levels in Industrialized, Market Economies and the Less Developed Countries

Estimates of Divergence of Per Capita Incomes (in dollars) Since 1870*

	1870	1960	1990
Per capita income in USA	$2063	$9895	$18054
Per capita income in world's poorest nation	$250	$257	$399
Ratio of GDP per capita of richest to poorest nation	8.7	38.5	45.2
Ratio of average "advanced capitalist" nations to average of all other nations	2.4	4.2	4.5

* Using 1985 purchasing power parity dollars

Source: Lant Pritchett, "Divergence, Big Time," *Journal of Economic Perspectives*, Summer 1997, p. 11.

Some Reasons for Divergence:

1) Lower Saving and Investment Rates in Poorer Nations

2) Faster Population Growth in Poorer Nations

3) Political and Economic Instability in Poorer Nations

4) Restrictions on Business and International Trade in Some Poorer Nations

ACTIVITY 1

 From Master Curriculum Guide in Economics: *Teaching Strategies for International Trade*. 1988. Joint Council on Economic Education. New York, NY.